R A

YOUR KIDS

WITHOUT

LOSING

YOUR COOL

RAISING YOUR KIDS WITHOUT LOSING YOUR COOL

SHANTELLE BISSON

DUNDURN
TORONTO

Publisher: Scott Fraser | Acquiring editor: Kathryn Lane | Editor: Jess Shulman
Designer: Laura Boyle
Cover images: istockphoto.com/ptasha
Printer: Marquis Book Printing Inc.

Library and Archives Canada Cataloguing in Publication

Title: Raising your kids without losing your cool / Shantelle Bisson.
Names: Bisson, Shantelle, 1969- author.
Identifiers: Canadiana (print) 20200156241 | Canadiana (ebook) 20200156276 | ISBN 9781459746305 (softcover) | ISBN 9781459746312 (PDF) | ISBN 9781459746329 (EPUB)
Subjects: LCSH: Child rearing.
Classification: LCC HQ769 .B57 2020 | DDC 649/.1—dc23

We acknowledge the support of the Canada Council for the Arts and the Ontario Arts Council for our publishing program. We also acknowledge the financial support of the Government of Ontario, through the Ontario Book Publishing Tax Credit and Ontario Creates, and the Government of Canada.

VISIT US AT

 dundurn.com |  @dundurnpress | dundurnpress | dundurnpress

Dundurn
3 Church Street, Suite 500
Toronto, Ontario, Canada
M5E 1M2

This book exists because of you, Brianna, Dominique, and Mikaela. Without you, I never would have lost my cool at times — actually, who am I kidding — often *daily*. I'm thankful that you always forgave me, that we always worked it out, and that we've ended up each other's favourite people. I love you, thank you for this book, and remember: "Life is both simultaneously too long and too short to spend it not living your passion."

Love, Your mom

Contents

Introduction

SO, MAYBE YOU'VE SEEN ME on TV discussing parenting. Perhaps you've read my blog and my online contributions to *Huffington Post* and *Everything Zoomer*. Now the critical moment is upon you. You're standing in the parenting section of the store with my book in hand. You've checked out my photo and you've read the little blurb about what you can expect within the pages. It's decision time. Do you buy my book or not? You speed-read through my bio one more time. "Her bio is unimpressive," you say to yourself. "She doesn't have a degree in child education, psychology, family therapy — any of it. What makes her an expert? Why should I listen to her?"

I'll tell you the single most powerful reason:

I am a survivor.

I am the mother to not one, not two, but *three* daughters.

I have lived through tween puberty and adolescence *three* times.

I have weathered and counselled them through brutal breakups.

I have sheltered them from bullies who just wouldn't quit.

I have raised the first generation of social media children and managed to get all three of my girls to adulthood without one of them baring their boobs for some boy to screenshot and send around the globe.

> Being a parent is like being on the front line of a war, every single day.

I am a parenting survivor.

Being a parent is like being on the front line of a war, every single day. And if you were going into an actual battle, who would you take with you? Someone who theorizes about battle? Or someone who has actually survived it?

I know who I would take.

Let me tell you, I wasn't the sort of woman who daydreamed about being a mother. I wasn't the doll-toting kind of kid. I was more of a climb-the-tree-with-my-big-brother-and-all-his-friends sort of girl. From a very young age, I had a vision for my life. I was put into dance class at the tender age of four, and from the first time the footlights shone upon my smiling face and people clapped, I was bitten. I knew right then and there that I would be a performer. As the years went by and I went to the movies and watched glamorous women in film and television, I was determined to become one of them.

Being a mother truly never crossed my mind. Not ever. I have not one single memory of envisioning my life with a husband or babies as part of the equation.

But the universe had another plan, and there I found myself, nineteen and pregnant, with a boy I didn't know I would love for thirty-two years, three daughters later. The odds were stacked heavily against us. We had been dating for only four months when we figured out we were expecting a baby. We were both from broken homes, both of us neglected by our parents — him by both parents, having been left to live on his own in pursuit of an acting career at the tender age of fifteen (regardless of what a child wants, a parent still needs to parent and guide their child); and me by a father who had no idea how to be in a relationship with a female if it wasn't sexual. My mother, a single parent, did all she could to give me a normal life and make up for the fact that my dad was not interested in me.

So, picture these two nineteen-year-old people, who barely know one another, procreating. Yeah. Wouldn't seem to be a hope in hell that we could work it out.

Yet we did.

Not only did we manage to stay together, thirty-two years and counting, but we have managed, despite all our baggage, our dysfunction and the lack of example set before us, to raise three of the most well-rounded, sensitive, intelligent, bold, talented, fearless women you've ever met. Not perfect, as we all know there's no such thing, but solid, respectful, caring global citizens.

We did a really great job, with few to no skills, even though we were young; even though it looked from the outside as if we would crash and burn and become just another group of statistics. Somehow, we were like the tributes in *The Hunger Games* — someone said, "May the odds be ever in your favour," and they were.

But how?

How did we manage to raise three incredible grown-up people, who happen to be three of our favourite people on the planet, without losing our cool? Well, those secrets are tucked into the pages of this book. I'm giving them to you.

> You're not *always* going to love your kid in the moment. But you *will* always love them.

I'm giving them to you, because this trend of helicopter and permissive parenting that is permeating our society is, pardon me for saying, fucking up our world. And it's pissing me off. It needs to stop. From when our first child (now thirty-one years old) was little to when our third child (now twenty-three) came along, parenting seemed to have become more permissive. And I know the trend has continued since. Now we have kids who don't know how to accept defeat, failure, or the word *no*. This is a huge problem. Kids need to know how to lose. They need to know how to accept *no* as a complete answer.

Not many parenting books will encourage you to discipline, or to stay out of your kids' relationships with their teachers or their classmates. Nor are any of your girlfriends going to tell you the whole truth and nothing but the truth about pregnancy, delivery, and the state of your post-baby vag.

But I will.

I will also tell you right here, right now, that you're not *always* going to love your kid in the moment. But you *will* always love them.

You won't always be thankful that you had them when the shit is hitting the fan. But in the end, they will become your favourite people.

My book will give you the tools you need to get through all the challenges of being a parent without losing your cool.

You can trust me on this. I've gone to battle, and I've won the war.

Chapter One

It Begins ...

LET ME BEGIN BY congratulating you on the impending arrival of your bundle of joy. All the clichés are true: a
child will add so much to your life. But you know this
already. You've watched your friends bring children into
their lives. You've watched hundreds of movies in which
two people fall in love, get married, have a child, and live
happily ever after. Maybe you're just one of those people
whose maternal instincts kicked in with your first baby
doll. But however, and whenever, parenthood began for
you, your journey now starts in earnest. For that, I send
blessings of good health to you, your unborn baby, and
your marriage, relationship, or partnership.

Let me address the elephant in the room: having kids
is not all fun and games. Children are not all rainbows
and butterflies. This is the biggest job you'll ever have and

the learning curve is steep, but you've got this. You will be an amazing parent. The fact that you're reading books, getting help in advance of your baby's arrival, proves it. Great parents are humble parents. Seeking help in an area that you know nothing about shows humility and responsibility and wisdom.

Yay, you!

Babies are giant lumps of responsibility and work. They are energy-sapping beings — beings you know nothing about. Believe me, as much as you may know, you know nothing until that baby appears. How to hold it, when to hold it, how long to feed it, when to put it to sleep, how long it should sleep in your room … the list is never-ending. People might tell you your instincts will guide you, but I've found that solid input and advice is just as (if not more!) useful. There will be more things that you do *not* know than you *do* know; things about this stranger in your home that you won't know until you get there.

And that's okay.

There will be many beautiful moments that you'll wish would never end, and there will be nights that you'll wish were already over. Wherever you are, whenever you get there is totally normal. Promise me that you will take it one moment at a time, give yourself grace, and love — lots and lots of love. Don't forget this. Promise. Keep in mind that it is totally normal to feel anxious about your impending role as a parent. Some of us may have had incredible role models in our own parents, but others may not have been so lucky.

Regardless of how you feel or think about what you experienced in your own life before this moment, open yourself up to what you don't know. We all look to what was done to us in our own childhoods and keep some things and throw away others. We may look to our own parents as models of our parenting ideals, or as examples of what not to do. Even with a rough idea about the kind of parent you will be, there is still much you won't know when it comes to taking care of this new little person. It is a truly scary prospect. Why do you think there are so many books out there telling you what to expect? It's because what we don't know freaks us out, and every baby is totally different. Every family is totally different, and every new parent is totally different. No baby comes with a manual. There's no test that you can study for where you'll either pass or fail, to determine whether you're going to be good at raising your kid. Much of parenting is learning on the job, and this job requires you to switch gears pretty much every minute of every day. As soon as you have baby figured out, they start teething and stop sleeping. Or they roll over for the first time while you're in the kitchen making a cup of tea and they roll themselves right off the couch onto the (carpeted, if you're lucky) floor.

Yeah, that happened. Learn from me. Don't leave a baby unattended on a piece of furniture, ever.

Basically, I'm going to be completely, and sometimes embarrassingly (for me), honest with you about where I failed as a mom. I'll share some of my victories and my losses, hopefully to help you mitigate your own. Essentially, this book and I are your manual.

Have you ever put together IKEA furniture, using the sketchy half-assed instructions they come with? You know, all the pieces are there, they all seem familiar, but there's no language in the directions: just a tiny line-drawn person putting screws into holes. You, the builder, are following along as best you can, banging it all together. You hope that in the end, you will have a shelving unit that will actually *hold* the weight of the books you want to put on it. Inevitably, there are leftover screws that you have no idea what to do with, so you shove those into a drawer and hope for the best.

Being a parent is a lot like that. You've got this little human in your hands, and you're a human, so you sorta know what this new one needs. But it's not as if you recall being that small, so how can you know if you're feeding it enough? How will you know if it's warm enough? Cool enough? How will you know anything about your baby? You can't talk to one another. You just sort of keep putting the screws in the holes, just like your IKEA furniture. You hope you're doing it the right way and that any leftover screws won't matter.

> Making a baby is the one time we get to actively partake in the creation of a miracle, so enjoy it.

And that's okay.

The truth is, you are probably equal parts nervous and excited about having this baby. If you were to be totally honest with yourself (or the person closest to you), chances are you would tell them that you're pretty freaked out about the whole thing.

You wonder: how is my life going to be different? And the answer is *totally*. It will be totally, completely different.

And that's okay, too.

Because the cool thing is that it will be different in so many groovy ways you can never imagine. Like being awake in the middle of the night while the rest of the city sleeps. Those are the moments that allow for amazing, undistracted, uninterrupted bonding time with your baby, who, believe you me, will be moving out before you know it. So, if you're freaking out about how much your life is going to change, or whether you'll be a good parent, relax. You can, and should, decide to just take this time of your life day by day, season by season. Making a baby is a miracle. It is the one time we get to actively partake in the creation of a miracle, so enjoy it. Celebrate it. Remember the miracle of it even when you're freaking out.

But let me say this — and I will come back to it later — you are *participating* in a miracle. This is not the same thing as giving life to the next Messiah. You're not the only person on the planet to make a baby, so please don't behave like it. And please don't treat your child as if it's the only living miracle. 'Cos it's not. Billions have come before your baby, and hopefully, if we can get a handle on this global-warming thing, billions more are yet to come. So, slow down and regain your cool right here and now.

The way my husband, Yannick, and I found out that we were pregnant was pretty funny, and it forced me to slow down instantaneously. I was nineteen. I had been well on my way to becoming a bit of a party girl. I'd graduated from high school with honours, but made no plans for a post-secondary education. Instead I was travelling and working a couple of jobs while trying to get my acting career off the ground. During this self-discovery hiatus from my education, I started dating a fellow actor, Yannick Bisson. He was quite successful and had lived on his own since he was fifteen. He was Mr. Independent, well on his way with his life plan. He lived with two other actors who, like me but unlike Yannick, worked in the restaurant business. Unlike me, my new boyfriend and his roommates liked to party. I hadn't even touched a drop of alcohol until I was eighteen, whereas plenty of kids I had been in school with were spending many nights on basement bathroom floors. When I started dating Yannick and hanging with older people, my partying escalated, which I believe could have led me down a not so great path. Luckily for my well-being, it wasn't long before I discovered I was pregnant, only a few months into dating him. That stopped me dead in my tracks. My life was changed forever, and for the better.

I remember my first thoughts very clearly. "When was the last time I smoked a cigarette? When was my last drink? Have I done any drugs while I was pregnant?" I was also concerned because I had just been at an amusement park with a girlfriend days earlier, riding all the roller coasters multiple times. How pregnant was I?

Well, it turned out that when I had ridden the roller coasters, I was already ten weeks pregnant! By the time I took a pregnancy test, I was eleven weeks along, and when I had my first ultrasound, I was thirteen weeks pregnant. I know you're asking yourself, "How did she not know she was expecting until she was ten weeks along? Is she dumb?"

No, I am not dumb. And if you don't realize you're pregnant right away, you're not dumb, either. If you have uneven menstrual cycles, and especially if you aren't actually trying to get pregnant, it's easy to miss. I had two periods and didn't really begin to think something was up until everywhere I went, I was falling asleep standing up, and I developed extremely tender breasts and a little paunch in my midsection. I was an actress and dancer who had never had a belly in her entire life, so before my next period was due, Yannick and I finally did a home pregnancy test. The test screamed at us, "What are you, stupid? Of course you're pregnant!" It was literally turning positive while I was peeing on it. Okay, well, not *while* I was peeing on it, but it went positive before I could even lay it on the counter. There was no waiting involved. We were pregnant. And life got really serious, really fast.

It probably did for you, too. The moment you discover you're pregnant, or you learn that you're finally going to be able to bring home a child by whatever means, everything in life becomes of consequence. It doesn't matter if it was planned and thought out, if you waited for your baby for many years, or if it took you entirely by surprise: the reality of having or getting a baby is scary, life-changing shit. You will have temporary moments of "what am I doing here?" and "what have I gotten myself into?"

And that's okay.

It's normal to wig out when the dream of parenthood finally becomes a reality. Lucky for you, I'm going to be your new best friend, unlike your other "best friends," who didn't tell you the whole truth and nothing but the truth. I'm actually going to pass on all the wisdom I've gained and lessons I've learned through thirty-one years of parenthood.

So, where do you begin? (We'll begin at the beginning.)

What do you need to make your house into a home? (I've got some ideas about what you do and do *not* need.)

What can you expect from this new person who will be moving in with you and your significant other? (Plenty, and nothing, at the same time — if that makes any sense at all.)

Here goes.

FIND A GREAT DOCTOR OR BIRTHING PRACTITIONER

First things first.

If you haven't already done this, get a great doctor or birthing practitioner — one you feel comfortable saying anything to or asking anything of. Make sure you can discuss the most intimate things imaginable with them. For example, "My husband, in my opinion, has a very large penis; how long can I continue to have sex with him?" Things that your friends can't tell you. Even I can't tell you that. I'm not a doctor and I've never seen said penis. A doctor is the best person to answer questions about how long it's safe for you to continue having sex.

> A good doctor can walk you through all the things the books and your girlfriends will never tell you.

You might have less important questions, like, "Why is it that sometimes when I sneeze, I also shart?" Now, this I can answer from experience. It's because there's a tiny human taking up all the space where your organs used to live freely. Now they're being squeezed by your baby, and sometimes things slip out when they're not meant to. Essentially, there just isn't room for all of it up in there, at least for now. A good doctor, one you have a strong, comfortable relationship with, can walk you through all the things the books and your girlfriends will never tell you. Things like the 99 percent chance you will poo on the table while you deliver. I did.

And that, if you deliver vaginally without an epidural, you will never, ever be prepared for the amount of pain that you will feel. In fact, I have many girlfriends who did have an epidural and still speak of unimaginable pain before the effects of the epidural kicked in. Here's the thing you're probably learning as you get deeper into your journey. Everybody has a ton of opinions — just like everybody thinks it's totally cool and all right to put their hand on your belly when you're growing your human. Excuse me, would you walk up to me and just touch my stomach if I wasn't pregnant? We all know the answer to that. No, you would not. Anyway, back to my original point: you've probably already learned that everybody wants to give you advice now that you're showing, or now that they know the arrival date of your adopted or surrogate baby. To those of you who are pregnant, some will tell you to absolutely *get the epidural*. And some will tell you that you don't need it, that it all actually goes by extremely fast and you won't remember it anyway, so go the natural route. To that I say: they don't live in your body. They don't know your pain threshold; you might be like me and be able to dance on a sprained ankle for three weeks, doing eight shows a day. Or you might be the sort of person who has to take an oxycodone and lie in bed for days after stubbing your toe. Only you know what you can or cannot handle in the pain department, so the decision is entirely, exclusively, your business and the business of your partner. To epidural or not epidural, that is the question.

So, as you're new to all this, let me give you some information about epidurals, or the pros and cons of them, if you will. The side effects can be merely inconvenient, such as itching, nausea and vomiting, fever, or a sore back for a few days in the place where they stuck the needle (which looks big enough to vaccinate a horse). Or there can be rarer, yet more serious complications. Sometimes the anesthetic can cause your breathing to slow. If they get the shit into your veins, it can cause seizures. If they're having an off day, they can slip and nick your spinal cord, causing a severe headache, or temporary or even permanent loss of feeling in your lower body.

Yeah, no thanks. When I read about all the possible side effects, I had a super-stern talk with myself. It went something like this: "Bitch, nothing lasts forever. This includes the pain of delivering your babies. Take a Tylenol 3, or a Demerol if you must, but do *not* go for this epidural shit." And so I didn't. And maybe, just maybe, if you've got yourself an awesome holistic adviser you can have honest conversations with, you can ask what they know about reducing pain with little or no risk to you or your baby, during what is undoubtedly going to be the worst agony you ever experience in five lifetimes. I've heard rumours that water births are virtually painless. (I say "rumour" because I've pushed three humans out of my body and don't see how that could be even remotely possible …)

Another fun fact: you will believe that your vag is never going to be the same again. For a few weeks, your greatest fear will be that the sandpapery feeling between your legs will be your vag's new normal. That it will never again be a place where fun happens. I'm here to tell you it does go away, and the fun will return to it again. I promise you this. You have my word.

But do me a favour, after you deliver your baby, go and smack all your girlfriends who didn't tell you just how bad the pain would be. Those nasty bitches should have been more upfront with you, like I'm being now.

> If you know what to expect — *really* expect — you can be prepared for it.

The truth is ugly, but freeing. If you know what to expect — *really* expect — you can be prepared for it. I prepared for it by taking Lamaze birthing classes and choosing a doctor who delivered in a hospital with a birthing centre. This centre had options for water births and allowed me to decide how many people I wanted in my birthing room with me. The room was also private, and I stayed there from the beginning stages of labour all the way to delivery. Barring any complications, this too can happen for you. The Lamaze classes enabled me to deliver all three girls without the need for an epidural, although this was mostly because when my water broke each time, my labour still never started on its own. I would just lie there, or walk around, until the time ran out. Eventually, the baby would be in there for too long without enough amniotic fluid, and then I'd be induced.

Let me tell you a little bit about being induced. Shit happens very fast once they put you on that drip, a.k.a. Pitocin. So fast in my case that, in fact, there was no time for an epidural even if I'd wanted it. There were a few times when contractions were rolling one over the other, seemingly with no end in sight, putting me in so much pain that I wanted to a) murder Yannick, b) rip the baby out of my body myself, c) get the fucking epidural! But the thing that saved me and allowed me to stick with my original plan to not risk an epidural was that my contractions, even on Pitocin, were slow to build, which meant I was also slow to dilate. It all seemed quite lovely … until it wasn't. And by the time it wasn't, I was too dilated, too close to pushing, to change my Lamaze-loving mind. Once you're close to pushing, the labour and delivery nurses want you to be able to be an active participant. I was so close that the epidural would have been setting in after the baby was already out. So at the birth of every daughter, it was just me, the Demerol, the contractions, and my convictions, and guess what? I survived.

Every pregnancy is different, just like every human being is different. However your baby comes to you is all good, whether it's via a vaginal birth or Caesarean, surrogate or adoption. The result is the same: you now have a baby, and that's amazing.

Your first homework assignment, as I said, is to do your research and find a fab doctor or birthing practitioner, who can be a midwife, a doula, a Lamaze coach, or whoever resonates with you and gives you confidence in your birthing journey. Choose someone who shares your philosophies on how and where to bring a life into this world. Maybe you want to give birth in a hospital or birthing centre or, hell, maybe even at home in a kiddie pool, like Kourtney Kardashian. Pick your birthing poison, my friends, so that you will be as physically and emotionally comfortable as you possibly can.

PLEASE DON'T DRINK WHILE PREGNANT

To me, this next piece of advice seems like a no-brainer, but I'm going to address it just to be on the safe side. There are a lot of varying opinions on this. In Europe, many women think nothing of a glass of wine or a beer every day while pregnant. Some women even believe that beer post-delivery helps with milk production. I'm not a beer drinker even on the hottest summer day, so I can't weigh in on whether this is actually fact. If you enjoy a little alcohol in your life, like I do (I'm no teetotaller), I will ask you to do this one little thing: please don't drink while pregnant. Let me repeat this. *Please* don't drink while pregnant.

Alcohol is a known teratogen, an agent or factor that causes malformation of an embryo. We know the detrimental effects of alcohol on the fully formed adult brain; just imagine what it can do to your baby's brand-new, just-beginning-to-develop brain. The verdict is still out as to how much alcohol actually causes fetal alcohol spectrum disorder (FASD) in an unborn baby. We don't know if it's a drink a day, two a day, one a week, two a week … There are no proven facts. So, if we don't have these stats, *why would you risk it at all?* You get only one chance to make a healthy baby.

The effects of FASD can include physical, mental, behavioural, and learning disabilities. Even without drinking, there's a chance your healthy kid could end up with obsessive compulsive disorder or attention deficit hyperactivity disorder (ADHD) or any number of other challenges. Do you really want to increase the odds? For me, this falls into the same category as the epidural. It's such a short moment in your life; are the potential side effects for your unborn baby really worth the momentary relief or enjoyment you'll get from the occasional glass of wine? Of course, I can't answer that for you. I can and did answer it for myself, but if you're unsure, just do your homework. Research the issue, seek advice from those who know, and make your choice. But I will say this: most of you didn't have your first drink until you were in your late teens, right? If you went all those *years* without a cocktail or a glass of wine, what's nine *months*? Honestly. Do your baby a favour and put down the glass.

The Institute of Medicine sums up why I chose not to touch alcohol during my pregnancies: "Of all the substances of abuse (including cocaine, heroin, and marijuana), alcohol produces by far the most serious neurobehavioral effects in the fetus."

This has been a Public Service Announcement. Thank you.

TIME TO ADOPT A HEALTHY LIFESTYLE

Throughout my career of nosily watching other people, I have found there are two times in life when people tend to really make their health a priority: 1) when they're getting married, and 2) when they're getting divorced. I implore you to add one more time in your life when your health should be your number one priority: when you're planning on becoming a parent. Even if you're not the person actually carrying the child, I don't want you to skip over this section. I want to really emphasize that. Even if you're adopting, that's not a get-out-of-jail-free card. Being a parent requires you to be healthy, for so many reasons. For example, you won't be sleeping all that much for the first year of your baby's life, give or take. Being well enables you to combat the kinds of illnesses that often come with being fucking exhausted. Then there are the illnesses you can pick up once they're off to nursery school or kindergarten. They will get germy, they will bring home many bugs, and you need to be ready for it — mentally and physically.

These are just the most obvious reasons. Somebody needs to nurse the sick kid, keep the house in check, and make the money. Trust me when I tell you that you cannot do any of these things if you don't take care of your own wellness *first*. So, do yourself a favour: be healthy, so you can stay healthy.

Another reason to begin focusing on your health Before Baby Arrives (or, as we will refer to it, BBA) is that you will have less time for yourself the moment they come home. Once you have a little human as your first priority, everything else takes a distant second place. So, make sure you start on this road to excellent health long before you actually get pregnant or bring baby home. Today is a great day to begin a new, healthier lifestyle. You might read this as, "Oh well, she says to get healthy *before*, but I'm already pregnant, so I'm too late. I'll get to it after the baby arrives." Or you might think, "I'll get my wellness in check before the next one." I've seen many, many people go this route, and I will tell you that it is *not* pretty. I advise doing it *now*, not later. Even if you're already months along in your pregnancy, it is never too late to stop where you are and begin new habits. Getting in shape and healthy after your baby is born is about a thousand times more difficult than just getting on top of that shit now. I might be exaggerating just a smidge (I don't know that it really is *one thousand* times harder), but it will be significantly more challenging — and discouraging — to try to get healthy or in shape with an extra 25 lbs on you. God willing, you might be lucky and gain *only* that much weight. I gained 50, 65, and then 80 lbs with my girls, so take my advice, get the weight off now. Change your lifestyle today. It will make losing the weight after giving birth so much easier.

This applies to dietary changes as well. It's no different from exercise. If you haven't already been taking care of your eating, now is as good a time as any to start. You will need mega-nutrients to get you through pregnancy, nursing, and, more importantly, through all the sleepless nights you will soon have. Notice how I keep talking about sleepless nights and health? That's because they go hand in hand. If you're not getting enough sleep, your immune system is challenged, making you susceptible to illness. You need to build up your ability to combat that as best you can. You need to get out in front of it by putting the work in *before* the sleepless nights become your new normal. Believe me, there is no adapting to it while it's happening!

The best comparison I can draw is to take you back to your party years, when you would stay out all night long, grab three hours of sleep, then go to work. Remember how you could do it for days on end — until finally the shit would hit the fan, and you'd land flat on your face in bed for days? Do you also recall how living that way eventually led you to some sort of ailment? Well, it's the same thing with a newborn baby living in your house, minus the flashing lights, excessive amounts of alcohol, and one of your girlfriends crying about her latest breakup.

To cope, you need sleep, nutrition, and exercise prior to your new person moving in with you.

Again, it doesn't matter whether you give birth to your new family member or adopt them: good nutrition is at the root of managing stress. And there will be stress. As much joy as those little bundles bring into your life, they bring equal parts stress. To cope, you need sleep, nutrition, and exercise prior to your new person moving in with you. You will want every tool available to combat any illness and manage your stress. Give yourself the gift of good health before your new roommate arrives.

Listen, no matter who you are — whether or not you're Beyoncé and essentially have an ATM in your kitchen and can afford the best of everything under the sun — we all have this in common: mothering begins on the inside. So, start taking care of yourself *now*, today, because somebody else's life depends on it. As do the lives of your future grandkids.

I told you this was the biggest job you'll ever have. It transcends your baby and continues into future generations. Isn't it cool to know that this one choice you make has such a huge impact on the future? It's awesome and super badass and powerful.

Yay, you!

When our youngest was a competitive cheerleader, I would sit in the stands to watch her practices from time to time, but not very often. Here's the main reason why: for the entire three hours that their children were being thrown fifteen feet in the air, tumbling their little asses off, doing double back tucks, front flips, whatever all that wild gymnastics business is technically called, many of the other parents sat and complained about their own lives. They had no time to eat right. They hadn't exercised in weeks, or months. They had high blood pressure. They had insomnia. And man, did they ever seem proud of it, too. It was as if their struggles to maintain a healthy lifestyle were linked to how much time they devoted to their "precious child." As if the sicker they were, and the less attention they paid to their own well-being, the better parents they were.

No, people. That's fucked up, and backward. Ignoring your health and not taking care of yourself doesn't make you a better parent. It actually makes you an incredibly selfish, lazy parent.

Don't do this. Don't become that mom who is *so dedicated* to her child that she gives up her own health so her kid can be extremely sporty, fit, and healthy. That's completely counterproductive and backward. Am I right?

I'd like you to take two minutes to think about why not taking care of yourself isn't a good idea.

You have, in your couple of minutes of silence, deduced (I'm sure) that your kid needs you to be healthy so you can be your best *you*. Your kid needs you to be healthy so you can take care of them. Don't let yourself go so that your kid ends up having to take care of you. You owe it to your child to be healthy. Start now. Begin shifting toward a much healthier lifestyle BBA. Your child will thank you for it. Your body will thank you for it. Your partner will thank you for it and so will your sex life. You're with me on this, right?

> You owe it to your child to be healthy.

Getting healthy doesn't mean you need fancy kitchen equipment — just buy better food. Eat more fresh food: eat salad instead of pizza for lunch. You don't need tons of money to take great care of yourself; you just need to decide to take better care, one meal at a time. You also don't need a gym membership to work out. All you need are your own two feet. Just start somewhere. Why not start at the beginning, one step, one bite, at a time? There are all sorts of apps to help you on your new journey, even some super-cool free ones. There are great home workouts on YouTube. Many don't even need any kind of equipment: just you and a pair of sneakers. Take the time to put your wellness first! You won't regret it if you do, but you might regret it if you don't. And here's one more little bit of encouraging information to assist you in seeking fitness BBA. The stronger your body is, the fitter you are, the easier your labour, delivery, and recovery will be. Who doesn't want those perks, if all it requires of you is a little hard work now?

(Maybe you do have an ATM in your house. Yay, you! You're lucky. If you really are fortunate enough to not have financial pressures and worries, then you have zero excuses for not being your best you already. But in the event you've been so busy building or running your empire that you've let your personal wellness slide, now is the time to get to it. With your financial freedom, you have the ability to take your wellness one step further. If you're not there yet, go organic, get a nutritionist, get a personal trainer: you can afford it, so just do it. Then follow the advice above that I gave to everyone else: those who, like me, do not have an ATM in their home. Chop-chop, friends; no time like the present!)

This isn't a licence to carry on an unhealthy relationship with food, either. If you've ever struggled with anorexia or bulimia, as I did (I was bulimic in my teens), or if you've been a yo-yo dieter — really, if you have any body or food issues at all, pregnancy can reignite them. Make sure you're deeply honest with yourself about your eating habits, and share that honesty with your partner and your doctor. If you feel yourself heading down that slippery slope, get help, pronto. Do not wait. Despite what the *Daily Mail* tells you, pregnancy isn't a competition in which you attempt to gain the least amount of baby weight ever. It's about being responsible and honouring yourself and your growing family by taking care of yourself. You with me on this? I'm not telling you to diet while pregnant — that's not at all what I'm saying. I'm telling you to have balance in your life: balance with your exercise, and balance with your eating.

Get used to this word. *Balance* shows up a lot in this book.

You should be making great use of this BBA time to get to know yourself better. Use the time to slow down, to *live life* rather than simply run through it. Take the opportunity, while you wait for your tiny human to join you, to go somewhere you've always wanted to go. Finish a project around your house that has been sidetracked because of your busy life. Read more. Sleep more. Live more. Connect more. As actor and comedian Eddie Cantor once said, "Slow down and enjoy life. It's not only the scenery you miss by going too fast — you also miss the sense of where you are going and why."

TO KNOW OR NOT TO KNOW, THAT IS THE QUESTION

I don't really have a strong opinion on whether you should learn the sex of your baby before it arrives. I do, however, have a strong opinion about these fucking gender-reveal parties. It's just my personal opinion, but *good Lord*. Come on. Please don't. Just don't. Go back in this chapter to where I said you're not the only person having a baby. You're not the first, you won't be the last, so just stop yourselves. This book is called *Raising Your Kids Without Losing Your Cool*. Having a gender-reveal party, as far as I'm concerned, puts you in such a "cool-bank" deficit that I honestly don't think you could climb out of it, no matter how many totally rock-star-cool things you did for the rest of your pregnancy. Some people tell me they want to have them just to celebrate with friends, simply get together and have a party. Okay, well, I have an idea: why don't you do what you used to do before you were pregnant and just have a goddamn party? Why does it need to be a gender-reveal party? Isn't that what showers are all about? Keep your cool, just be pregnant, and have a party if you want to have a party. Let's not do a gender-reveal party, friends. It's indulgent and absurd, so try to resist.

Okay, personal-opinion rant over; carrying on.

With our first, we didn't find out the gender, but we did with the middle, and the youngest. I have my reasons as to why I wanted to know, but I won't bore you with them. At the end of the day, don't let anybody judge you for whichever way you go on this topic. Find out, be surprised — do what you want to do. That's all I'm going to say on the matter. And remind you not to have a gender-reveal party.

GETTING YOUR HOUSE PREPARED BBA

In this day and age, where we willingly stand in line for hours for the newest, most updated iPhone so that we can be one of the first people to get the damn thing — even though we're currently holding a perfectly good six-month-old one in our hands — it's easy to convince ourselves that we need the newest, shiniest, most up-to-date version of everything. It's easy to get pulled into the belief that you need *everything*. And even easier to fall into the belief that your *baby needs everything.*

I have news for you. A baby doesn't really need all that much. Really. Mostly diapers, a small mountain of washcloths, some baby blankets, or swaddling blankets, if you're into those. Another small mountain of one-piece underwear or, depending on the climate where you live, half a dozen pairs of long PJs; a Baby Bjorn or some equivalent to strap them to you if they get fussy; a car seat for safe transport; and a stroller to keep you on track for that healthier lifestyle you've adopted. And that's it. Oh, and your boobs, if you're nursing, and if not, then some really high-quality, low-allergenic formula, and glass bottles to feed with.

I say glass because this way you can warm them in a pot on the stove rather than in a plastic bottle in a microwave, which … *eww*. Eww to the plastic and to the microwave. We all know about that industrial chemical, bisphenol A (BPA). Even if they say it doesn't exist in plastic bottles anymore, as a skeptical person, I'd rather not risk my child's health by warming up their formula in a plastic bottle in a microwave, and in fact I didn't. I only ever used glass bottles in a pot of boiling water on the stovetop.

But I digress; this is not about plastic versus glass, or microwaving or not microwaving. This is about what a baby needs, and as you can see the list is quite small, because they don't need all that much. So many people go crazy with adorable little newborn outfits that their baby either pees in or pukes on, usually the instant the clothes are put on. It's an unwritten rule: the nicer the outfit, the quicker your child will vomit on it. Or immediately have one of those poops that comes spraying out of the side of their diaper, staining the cute getup instantly. If you're lucky, as we were with our second daughter, your baby will sleep so many hours at a time that you can really cut down on the costume changes. Babies also grow out of clothes at the speed of light — practically from bath time to bedtime. So, save that money and put it into your baby's college fund. A fantastically cute outfit that baby can wear for fifteen minutes just isn't worth it. Like your new healthy-eating lifestyle, a college fund is something your baby will thank you for later.

End Rant 2.

As with everything about bringing a little human into your lives, I truly suggest you and your partner make a set of "need it," "can live without it," and "if only" lists together. It's a good starting point. Trust me on this. Your significant other will have a lot of thoughts, feelings, and ideas on how they want their baby to "live." Even when you think they are contentedly leaving you to make all the decisions, they will suddenly have a very strong notion about what they feel your baby should have.

You are probably asking yourself, "Didn't she go hog wild when she had her first baby?" The answer to that question would be "yes, a little bit." But we didn't have much money, so my go-hog-wild tendencies were severely restricted. Remember, we were nineteen. I kept my fingers crossed that my family would host baby showers so I could check off some of the more expensive items on my "if only ..." list. I suggest you do the same. Leave the larger-ticket items, such as highchairs or travel cribs, to the girlfriends who didn't tell you the truth about how painful childbirth really is. I mean, they sort of owe it to you, anyway.

Whatever you do happen to pick up for yourself along the way, do yourself a favour: bring your stash home and get organized, right away. Don't let it pile up to the point where you can't see the floor or your furniture. I had one girlfriend who did this. She was so completely overwhelmed with setting up the baby's room that she just didn't. So my youngest and I went to her house and got the entire room done in one afternoon, just days before her baby arrived. We did it quite happily because my youngest and I love to organize, and the problem with being an organized person is that once your own stuff or space or home is all organized, there isn't much more to do. A project like my girlfriend's was a dream for us type-A personalities! After all, not all people's brains work like ours. If yours doesn't, enlist the help of somebody who loves this kind of thing, whether it's someone close to you or someone you hire. And if you're like me and my youngest and love labelling shit, folding clothes, and colour-coding closets, then organize away!

Oh, and one more thing I'd like to add here. If you do have a baby shower, take the time to *thank* people for their lovely gifts. Don't be one of those people who can't take a few hours to write and send out thank-you notes. There are many other things people could be doing with a half-day on the weekend than spend it watching you open baby gifts, so please be thankful — outwardly, not just silently in your heart.

Let's continue.

Do the easy stuff first. Pick the paint colour for the baby's room. I recommend Benjamin Moore's Natura paint with zero volatile organic compounds. We painted our entire home with these paints; you can sleep in the room within hours. Have fun setting up the nursery, even if your nursery is inside your bedroom, tucked in a cozy corner. Put all the IKEA furniture together with all the super-helpful directions they come with. Take this time, BBA, to get that space ready to rock 'n' roll. Make that space all about the baby. Remember this will be the last time you'll bring your baby home for the first time, so make it something to treasure.

If you have a mountain of newborn clothes, now is a good time to wash, fold, and put them away in age-specific drawers. Put anything that is size three-to-six months or bigger in a clear bin in the baby's closet, to be used when your baby grows into them. This really helps with not grabbing the wrong size when packing your diaper bag. (And packing those extra clothes is critical — you'll need a change of baby clothes when you're at your in-laws' place and your baby poops up their back in the current cute outfit. Know that this will happen many times. It's always good to have many replacement outfits on hand when you're out for the day.)

Also, now is the time to pack your hospital bag. Pack it like you would for a beach holiday: light but with more than you might need. We all hope and pray that delivery will go well, that your baby will latch at the breast easily, and that you'll be home before you know it, but in the event there is any sort of delay at the hospital end, you want to have exactly what you need to be comfortable. They do rush you in and out of there quickly these days, so try to see if you can squeeze an extra twenty-four hours out of them. It really helps to have that extra day of sleep, expert support from the nurses, and recovery time before you get home.

With our first-born, Brianna, I went home the next day. Dominique, our second baby, had jaundice, so I was able to stay put for five days until she was cleared of it. Let me tell you, with a two-year-old waiting for me at home, and Yannick in New Zealand wrapping up filming on a project, those extra days and all the extra help I got from the nurses were like *heaven*. By the time our third daughter came along, I had a lot more knowledge under my belt, so I made sure that when I delivered Mikaela in Los Angeles, I knew exactly how many days my insurance would cover. Then I stayed in the hospital until they kicked me out. It was amazing.

A piece of advice: figure out how many days you're entitled to stay in the care of nurses who have delivered thousands of babies, and enjoy every minute of their knowledge and help!

Now is also a good time to do something special with your own sleeping space so that it still feels like a space for you and your partner, apart from your baby. Get a new throw blanket, switch out your bedding or your duvet, get fresh pillows. Rearrange your sentimental objects. Do something that feels like you're freshening up your own private space as well as creating one for the baby. I feel like I'm forgetting something. What am I forgetting?

Oh yeah: have sex.

THINGS TO NIBBLE ON

Get a great doctor or birthing practitioner, one you connect with, feel comfortable with, and trust, who shares your vision of how to bring your baby into this world. Make sure they work out of a hospital or birthing centre that practises the sort of delivery options you're interested in.

Adopt healthy eating habits, and if you're not already exercising, begin now by adding a program into your lifestyle, one approved by your doctor.

Whether or not you choose to know the gender of your baby is your business; don't let people pressure you one way or the other. But please, don't do the gender-reveal party, I'm begging you.

Don't overdo it on buying things for a baby; they need very little in the beginning. Get your baby's room ready and pack your hospital bag. And if you really, really want to go crazy, enlist the help of friends and family to purchase some of the bigger items for you.

Have sex!

Chapter Two
Decisions, Decisions

AWESOME. WE GOT A TON of shit checked off your list. You've picked the most amazing, wonderful doctor or practitioner. You've made the necessary lifestyle changes to set yourself up for the first six sleep-deprived, former-shell-of-yourself months (I promise it's temporary). You've decided whether to find out what flavour of baby you're getting, and you know that it's your business, and your business only. You're taking it easy on the binge baby shopping.

And I know you've totally taken me up on my suggestion to have sex, so let's move on, shall we?

With the arrival date fast approaching, it's time to get serious about making some parenting decisions. Having your thoughts together BBA is *essential* to making the new-baby-in-the-house transition go more smoothly. Now, you may be asking yourself, "How am I supposed to make decisions before I've done even a second of parenting? I've never been on this train!" Don't worry. You'll be making on-the-fly decisions every day from here on out. My point is that discussing certain things BBA, at least developing some sort of game plan, will make for a much easier transition.

PROMISE TO STAY COOL

I want to impart a little nugget of wisdom to you. I strongly suggest that you and your significant other decide on how you want your new family member to learn about the world. In recent years, I've witnessed two different types of new parents. (Even though all our girls are well into adulthood, I say "recent years" because remember that my hubby and I had our first kid at nineteen, when none of our friends were having babies yet. It wasn't until many, many, *many* years later that the people we hung out with started to have kids of their own.)

Let me tell you this: it is amazing to watch how differently people behave with their first-borns. One couple we knew brought their new daughter with them everywhere. Their mindset was: *she's part of us, we're a trio, she goes where we go*. I have to admit, there were times when this was annoying. Our own kids were grown and we were ready to socialize baby free. But, remarkably, having their tiny human at adult gatherings was pretty chill. The kid was not afraid of anything. She would gladly be handed from one set of hands to another. She would let our daughters cart her away from her parents to have her hair brushed, her baby nails painted, or just sit in the middle of a circle of dolls to play with. She couldn't have cared less what her parents were doing, ever. This began from the time she was six months old.

One specific moment of her uber-chillness comes to mind. She was sitting on our living-room floor, and our two big boxers were all in her business — sniffing her, licking her ears — and suddenly they knocked her over.

Her reaction? Laughter. She was a confident, mini–human rock star, who I can proudly say is now a totally groovy, bright, well-adjusted teen.

On the flip side, we had another set of friends who had a baby girl just two months after that first couple. Lives got busy and we didn't hang out all that much with them during their baby's early days. But they happened to come to a group celebration for something (I can't recall what), and we quickly saw that their method of child-rearing was quite different from that of our other friends with the ridiculously chill baby (they were also at this gathering). Let me tell you, the contrast between those two little girls was mind blowing. I was stunned to see the difference between the effect that being an overprotective parent, and a groovy, chill, trust-the-universe-and-let-your-child-*live* parent could have on a child. I had no personal experience with what is now called the helicopter parenting style, as we had always been allow-our-girls-to-walk-through-life-touching-feeling-tasting-it-for-themselves parents.

Yannick and I socialized our girls from a very young age. Brianna was younger than two when we moved to New Zealand, where we knew nobody, and the TV and film crew we were working with became like family to us. She grew up with adults. She was always on sets, and always travelling. The same can be said of our other two daughters. All three were socialized in primarily adult environments because we spent many years living far away from family when the girls were quite young. This, along with our "we're just going to be cool" attitude with them, encouraged them to behave respectfully in an adult world, and to engage with their environment in a way that didn't make the adults around them (or us) run for the hills or suddenly fake an illness if we invited them out with our family. In fact, it was quite the opposite, even though we were so damn young, and all three of our girls were the only children in any of our circles. Consequently, our girls were like party favours; our friends wanted to come over *all the time* to hold them, to chill with the living, breathing baby dolls. Holding a sweet, calm baby can be an instant blood-pressure reducer, and boy, do you forget about your day once you pick one up: perfect for my single, university-aged girlfriends who seemed to always be trying to forget about a horrible date or a bad breakup. Also, I come from a large family, and being far away from them meant we needed our village of friends to help us figure out what the hell we were doing with our first tiny human.

So, all three of them were socialized a great deal. That allowed us a tremendous amount of freedom, which also allowed us to enjoy them more. We were so relaxed because at just twenty years old, we didn't know any other way to be. Who knew that a fever of 104 degrees is ridiculously high and probably requires medical attention? We knew so little that it kept us from freaking out. Like the time we played "whoopee" with Brianna on a walk, each of us holding one wrist and on the count of three swinging her toward the sky, calling out "Whoopee!" Fun, right? She squealed, we laughed, she called out "Again! Again!" It was literally all fun and games until her shoulder popped out of its socket.

(Are you kidding me? That can happen when you play this totally fun, innocent, happy game with your kid? They do it in the movies all the time!)

We didn't know a lot of things. And the truth is that not knowing kept us pretty damn cool, which in turn created easygoing, happy, confident, independent girls, which caused us to be even more chill. And our bonus? Life was not that much different with them in it. So, trust me when I tell you this: do not make your life fit your baby. Make your baby fit your life.

Let's return to that party, and the two different babies being raised in two completely different ways. Baby 1 is chill, independent, and easygoing, because her parents have given her the freedom to learn the world on her own terms. She's having a ball. Her parents are also having a relaxed, groovy, lovely adult Sunday afternoon. Baby 2 … well, let's just say she is clinging to her mother *for dear life*. As though some way, somehow, in her tiny baby brain she just knows there is a child abductor in the crowd, and she is not safe. When the mom finally gets her daughter's death grip off her neck and passes her to the dad

> Do not make your life fit your baby. Make your baby fit your life.

to take over for five minutes so she can go pee or something, the dad brings her inside, where our boxers are — those same two knucklehead dogs who earlier gave Baby 1 a tongue-bath and accidentally knocked her over. I want to emphasize that Baby 1 was not hurt in *any* way when that happened; she just tumbled onto her ass. Anyway, moments later we have Baby 2 crawling around the floor in the boxer baby swap. Dad 2, after eyeing the boxers, who are both totally passed out, decided it was cool to let her crawl around for a little bit so he could sip his beer and chat with me while I tossed a salad — as he kept an eye on her the whole time, of course. After all, Baby 1 had just had a gay ol' time with the boxers and got to live another day.

Yeah, right.

The boxers heard her cooing around on the floor and wanted to nuzzle and lick her, just as they had with Baby 1. That is, until Baby 2 saw them coming toward her and let out a blood-curdling scream that made the dad almost drop his beer. I jumped out of my skin. I expected to see her severed arm or leg or something right there on the floor. Dad 2 reached down and grabbed her before either of our dogs could get anywhere near her. His face was white, the baby was screaming for dear life, and my boxers were laid flat out on their stomachs. The dad clutched his daughter, ran out to the backyard to his wife (who was finally relaxing a bit), and very shortly afterward, they all made a hasty retreat.

We haven't seen or spoken to them to this day. I kid you not.

What is the point of this rant of mine?

The point is this: even though you know they are fragile little beings, and you will always put their well-being at the top of your priority list, they're not made of glass. A few bumps and bruises along the way makes for a kid who won't collapse in a heap of hysteria whenever they trip and fall. Even though you will want to, you won't always be there to catch them. Let them fall so they learn how to get up again.

Now, it's possible to take this too far. When our middle girl, Dominique, was three years old, she went through this phase of intentionally trying to off herself. While we lived in New Zealand, at her actual third birthday party, which was a pool party attended by a good dozen kids, she decided to go against our instructions to keep her floaties on *at all times* while around the pool. She decided that day, the day of her birth, was a great time to test the hands of fate, and her swimming skills, and jump into the pool sans floaties. I was inside getting the buns for the hot dogs, Yannick was at the grill around the corner from the pool, and all the other moms were standing around, chatting. Brianna called to me for help, but as I watched Dominique's little head dip below the surface, I froze in place. I stood there, screaming. It was a quick-thinking ten-year-old boy, JP, who dived in and pulled her out. By now Yannick was on the scene. He grabbed her out of the little boy's hands while I dialled 911. They instructed us to hold her upside down and bang her on the back to get the water out of her lungs … and when she spat out water and started to cry, we would know there was a good chance she no longer had any fluid in her lungs.

That incident took a long time for all of us to get over. Admittedly, we had to face up to the fact that we had taken the "be cool" attitude a little far that day. Let's just say she never went into another pool without her floaties, despite taking swimming lessons (but she did start a trend of "allowing" herself to fall down a flight of stairs, all thirteen steps, three times in the span of one year. She's still with us. Thank God).

You're asking yourself, "Who doesn't have an eye on their kid at all times around a pool, or any body of water?" Lots of people, unfortunately, and of course it's a mistake. People who, like me, assume their child will obey the rules, and who assume that somebody else is paying attention when they themselves are not. That's an assumption I never made again. *Nobody else is going to raise or protect your kid.* That is your job. I almost learned that lesson in an irreversible way. I'm showing you my ugly warts so you will promise to take it easy on yourself, as well as your baby, so you can both enjoy one another as you protect them from harm without suffocating them with fear.

Oh yeah, and please do everybody in your life a favour: as I said earlier, you're not the only person on the planet to have a baby. Keep your social media posts down to a dull roar. We liked you much better when you were posting food photos, which isn't saying much but it was way better than a play-by-play of your child's development. We don't need to watch your new-parent journey unfold before our eyes every fifteen minutes. Your friends, family, and internet lurkers thank you in advance.

> Nobody else is going to raise or protect your kid.

You're a cool person. Your friends and family totally love you, they enjoy hanging out with you, they have done so for many years, right? Do yourself a favour, and keep being that cool person post-baby's arrival (or PBA). All right?

Are you going to promise me that you'll do that? Vow to yourself, your partner, your co-workers, your friends, your family, the planet, that you are going to keep your cool. This begins with having a discussion, and then making a decision, about what sort of parents you're going to be. Do you want to be the type who believe that the sky is falling? That the world, including your friend's party, is a place where your child could meet their demise? If you are, then I'm going to give you my frank opinion: do a solid for the future neurotic weirdo you're about to raise, and don't become parents. Parenting is a messy, learning-on-the-job position. It is a catch-your-breath-and-live-holistically role that requires flexible captains at the helm. If you can't be that person, don't apply for the job.

Oh, wait.

You've already accepted the job.

Shit, I forgot that tiny detail. Okay, well, as you've already accepted the job, may I just tell you this. For the love of God, society, and your kid, *keep your cool.*

If you haven't already had that "this is how I think children should be raised" conversation with your partner, I'm going to review the subject with you now, in an abbreviated version.

You and your partner come from two different backgrounds; you were each raised by two people, maybe more, maybe fewer. You may have racial or religious differences, maybe both. The point is you're different, and you were raised by different people. You most likely have very different ideas about what to do with your child. In my own life, both my parents remarried, but my mom was the primary caregiver. My mother didn't remarry until we all had long moved out. I didn't have too many cooks in my child-rearing kitchen, which I think is a good thing. You, on the other hand, might come from a throwback family. You know, the kind where your parents are still together and are more in love today than they were when you were little. Whatever your family history is, it influences you in ways you both know and don't know. Believe it or not, I've seen more couples have disputes over how they're going to raise their kids than over infidelity. Raising kids is a serious issue, one that you need to discuss right away. But if you haven't, and you've left it to the last minute, it's still okay. We're going to work out some boundaries, come to some agreements and compromises here, so that you and your partner can get on with enjoying, rather than fighting about, your baby.

FIGURING OUT THE SLEEPING ARRANGEMENTS

One very important piece of the how-will-baby-live puzzle is deciding on where and how they will sleep. Sit down with your partner and figure this out BBA, particularly if you are living in a small apartment, or some other tight space. Don't kick this decision down the field until the day your baby appears. You will both be operating under severe sleep deprivation, especially if you end up with a baby like our eldest, who would sleep for only one hour at a time, all day long. We were exhausted, to say the least. But we were only nineteen, so our youth saved us. On the other hand, our middle girl, Dominique, slept eight hours a night by the time she was three weeks old, and by the time she hit the ripe old age of six weeks, she was sleeping twelve hours. Mikaela, our youngest, slid in right in the middle, averaging about six hours straight for the first year. My point is, you don't know what kind of sleeper you'll get, but you'll more than likely be tired, so make sure you're organized on this point in advance.

Many people start with their baby next to them, in their bedroom in a bassinette, close enough to grab for those multiple middle-of-the-night feedings. Some will choose to put the baby into their own swanky nursery from the get-go, and others will opt for the family bed. All are fine options, although I'll get into why the bassinette-next-to-you route makes the most sense, at least for the first few months. And the last one does make me a bit nervous. A lot of professionals don't recommend it, in part for the very reason I don't like it: I personally would worry about rolling onto baby while in a deep sleep and smooshing them. There are people who do go this route, and it seems like we never hear about a crushed baby in the family bed, but it still isn't for me. In any event, I suggest that you get baby out of your bed ASAP. That bed is for you and your partner, to sleep, connect, and — as I said earlier, and will continue to harp on throughout this entire book — *to have sex in*. Unless you're okay with throwing it way back to high school and getting down on your couch or on the carpet in the TV room. But let's face it, once you're over thirty, the bed is the most comfortable. If you truly are okay with everybody being in your bed, then I suppose go ahead and keep your baby there until they go to university. I'm just going to stress that you make sure *both* you and your partner feel strongly about the family bed, if that is the choice you're making.

No matter where you're putting your baby to spend their (most certainly non-sleeping) nights, just make sure you and your partner are in 100 percent agreement. If you're not, then this is where the art of compromise comes into play, and for that I wish you good luck. Remember, this is the book about raising kids, not the one about managing your relationship; that's a totally separate, more in-depth book on how to not become a statistic.

Once you have the baby's sleeping location all worked out, you're probably going to wonder whether you need a monitor. There are tons of monitor options, from the very basic all the way to complicated, high-tech video monitors that let you see right into the crib and even talk to your baby. As I said in my opening, I'm not a doctor. Nor am I a scientist or an expert in the potential dangers associated with Wi-Fi, electromagnetic fields (EMF) or radio frequency (RF). The WHO (that's the World Health Organization, not the band) says there are no "known" negative health side effects associated with being surrounded by all the "low-radiating" objects that follow us everywhere, day in day out. But they do acknowledge that more research is needed to determine just what, if any, long-term side effects might exist, such as cancer. Our offices, our cars, our homes, where we dine: you name it, we're literally surrounded. I buy into the concern so much (that maybe these things could be altering my DNA or causing cancer) that I have our home Wi-Fi router on a timer.

"What does she mean, she has her Wi-Fi on a timer?" you're asking yourself.

It's just like when you go away on vacation and you want to trick any potential thieves into thinking you're actually home, so you plug a bunch of your lights into timers and *voilà*! the lights go on and off at the times you've set. This is what we do with our Wi-Fi every night. Even though the WHO says that a year near a Wi-Fi hot spot gives you the same radiation as a twenty-minute cellphone call, I'm still not playing with any of this shit. And my kids laugh at me for using the speaker phone for every single phone call I take on my cell. Honestly, I'd rather be wrong about it and alive than cavalier and, you know, dead. Listen, the bottom line is that Wi-Fi is here to stay. It's such a part of our everyday lives, it's at Starbucks, it's in the mall, it's on airplanes: it is literally everywhere. As I cannot control what is going on in the world around me, I choose to do what I can to limit my personal exposure inside my own home. Turning it off while I sleep is a great way to not have it around me for at least half the day ... I kid, I kid, I don't sleep twelve hours a night! I wish.

Because you're new to the parenting thing, and there are so many decisions to make right now BBA (this is why I'm here to help you out), may I share a concern that I have about the latest and greatest baby monitors? The bulk of them operate on the digital enhanced cordless telecommunications (DECT) system, which gives off a certain amount of radiation. "They" say it's a safe amount, but, I mean, it's still radiation ... and we willingly put these baby monitors right beside our kids' heads? You put the word *radiation* in any sentence and I'm not even going to listen to anything after that. I don't care if it's a minimal amount. Any appliance that gives you long-range reception with no cord is DECT. In a nutshell, DECT baby monitors operate on the same electromagnetic frequencies as your microwave (which you should get rid of, because why on earth would you eat *radiated* food? But that's a rant for another time), your Wi-Fi router and your beloved cellphone that you probably sleep with right next to your head, soaking yourself in EMF all damn night long. (I'll rant about sleeping with your cellphone later: you might as well put yourself inside the microwave and turn it on.) Seriously, folks, there are thousands of articles about the dangers of the radiation we receive all day long, from our wireless headsets, our cellphones, our laptops, our handy-dandy cordless mice and keyboards, and our microwaves. You wouldn't warm your breast milk in the microwave, right? ('Cos you really shouldn't — it ruins the milk.) Then why would you want to put your baby to sleep next to a baby monitor that's emitting those same EMFs?

For me, knowing that radiation comes off a baby monitor has me giving the DECT monitors a hard pass. The verdict is still out in the extremely heated debate as to whether any of these things interrupt the natural development of a baby's brain. In Europe they seem to think they do, so they're on the cutting edge of knocking down these potential dangers by making non-DECT baby monitors. As a mom of three girls, I say, *why the hell take the chance?* I'm not a gambler — I won't even put twenty dollars into a slot machine — so there's no way in hell I'm gambling with not only my kids' brains, but my own as well.

The truth of the matter is that babies cry loudly. Incredibly loudly. They let you know when they want or need something, so the monitor with the camera on it showing exactly how your baby is sleeping really is overkill. Besides that, I personally think those are a little *1984* of today's parents, but that's just my opinion. And as a mom who has been there and done that, I can assure you that once your baby is sleeping and your body hits your bed, you're fucking exhausted. So for all those parents who say, "I want to be able to hear it if my baby stops breathing," I'm going to be honest with you. Once you're asleep, you're not going to hear it if your baby stops breathing, not even on the most sensitive of baby monitors.

But this isn't a campaign to get parents to stop using baby monitors, let's get that straight right away. I used them with my girls. I'm just saying find one that isn't going to radiate the shit out of your brand-new little human.

I know the idea of sudden infant death syndrome (SIDS) terrifies you, as it should. The riskiest age for SIDS is reported to be between two and four months (and for some reason, the risk seems to be higher for male babies), and some literature even extends that age range all the way to one year. So if you want to do everything you can to give your baby the best chance against SIDS, here are some simple things the experts suggest:

1. Always put your baby to sleep on their back. This helps eliminate the potential for smothering when the baby is small and is not yet rolling over.
2. The firmer the mattress, the better. Also, as cute as it is to surround your baby with all the soft and cuddly

stuffies you've bought them, don't put them in the crib, at least until they're old enough to move away from one if it gets too close to their nose or mouth. All of the bedding should be tight-fitting, so there's no risk of a sheet coming off the mattress and getting tangled around them. (The experts even suggest not putting bumpers in the crib, or sheepskins ... we did both of these things with all of our girls. Good Lord, we were lucky!)

3. This one is a no-brainer: don't smoke around your baby.

4. My personal favourite — and do I feel vindicated when I see experts reinforcing my own opinion? Oh, yes, I do! — *don't let your baby sleep in your bed.* In the room? Yes. Very close by, so close you have to climb out of your partner's side of the bed to go pee in the middle of the night? Also yes. But in the bed? *No.*

5. If you are able, if your body works this way (mine didn't with my first), and only if you want to, breastfeed as long as you can. Experts aren't sure why, but babies who are not breastfed seem to have a higher risk of SIDS.

6. The use of pacifiers also reduces the risk of SIDS, but nobody knows why. Big help, right? Hey, I'm not the researcher. I'm just telling you what I've read. And what's the harm in following this advice? No harm at all.

7. Don't overdress your baby for sleeping. If you really need to show Instagram how adorable your baby is when it sleeps, then go for it, dress them to the nines

for the picture. But as much as you can, be sensible and dress them in a way that they won't overheat.

8. Don't drink alcohol while breastfeeding. Heavy alcohol consumption increases the risk of SIDS. If you are going to drink, it's advised that you pump your breast milk before drinking and feed that to baby. Then express your milk after consuming alcohol and throw that away. And that's the tea on SIDS. Use these tips to help reduce your baby's risk.

Listen, I get it. You just want to be the best parent you can be, and a baby monitor helps you fulfill that desire. I respect that. But if you start by making sure their sleeping setup is kosher, then you won't need to be staring at a monitor screen all night long when you're supposed to be sleeping.

So Big Brother surveillance isn't going to be your modus operandi, but you still really, really want a baby monitor. How about you just look into some non-DECT models? Do your homework, parents. Don't just follow the crowd down the path to technology-related illness. This is your *baby*. You research cars and appliances, right? So, take some time to sit down and explore the world of EMF, RF, and their link to cancer and brain development, draw your own conclusions, and buy your baby monitor accordingly.

When I see anything that's been identified as a "known carcinogen," I run for the hills. I listen to everybody's whack-a-doodle advice for combatting cancer. What's the worst thing that can happen if you don't own a microwave and you sleep with your Wi-Fi off, and your cellphone off and in another room? You'll feel better, you'll sleep more deeply, and hey, you'll quite possibly knock down your risk of getting cancer. Sign me *up*, I say! And when you sleep better, and feel healthier, guess what you're more likely to be in the mood for? You got it! *MORE SEX!*

Listen, I believe in this so strongly that I hired an EMF specialist to come through our home before we renovated to tell me if the house was worth keeping or if it was already over-radiated just based on its location. He assured me that the house was in a healthy location, but he gave us some wall filters from Germany to knock down the RF and the "dirty electricity" coming out of our sockets. In simple terms, electrical devices all draw different levels of electricity from the wall, and this creates spikes or surges of electrical energy that's sort of left over from the standard juice your system puts out. That energy, called "dirty electricity," spreads through your wiring, creating EMFs around your house. Multiple studies from Russia, Sweden, and Eastern Europe link high exposure to EMFs to migraines, ADHD, multiple sclerosis, and childhood cancers, just to name a few. Once again, I'd rather be wrong and not potentially fatally ill, than wrong and dead.

So we bought a boat-load of these filters and have them in every single outlet in our house. I have battery-powered alarm clocks and my cellphone stays outside my room, no matter what. If you need me, call me on the landline (which is plugged into the wall on the other side of my room). After we installed the filters, I had noticeably fewer headaches and my chronic fatigue went away, as did my foggy brain and the feeling like I was constantly "fighting something." All gone. It made me a believer. So much so that when we built a new home on that same property, I hired the specialist again to work with our designer on the electrical plans for our home and eliminate the ability of EMF to transmit around the home. (Honestly, I didn't believe it either when a girlfriend told me that this guy had changed her health, but I followed his advice, reduced my exposure to EMF by a ton, and it's made a world of difference.)

Even if you stop reading right here, even if you decide I'm some wacky conspiracy theorist, why not err on the side of caution? We get only one brain, and one life. Why wouldn't you be as careful as possible with your health and the health of your baby, and use a low-tech baby monitor?

Trust me, your baby will thank you.

So, now that you've decided where baby is going to sleep. What's next?

THE GREAT BREASTFEEDING QUESTION

Remember those really amazing girlfriends of yours who withheld how painful childbirth really is but then made it up to you by throwing you that ridiculously awesome baby shower, where you got all those cool gifts? Well, I'm here to tell you that they withheld something else from you.

Which is how much breastfeeding hurts, and how your breasts will grow as large as bowling balls, and just as hard, when you first start breastfeeding. They also didn't tell you how, when you hear any baby crying (and it doesn't even have to be *your* baby), your breasts will just start leaking breast milk everywhere. Which is fantastic for you working moms who could just be out during your lunch break, enjoying a healthy meal of veggies and good clean protein, when the baby at the table next to you starts crying, and bam! Your breasts are ready to save the day and feed that crying child. Yup. This will happen, so if you're breastfeeding, make sure you have plenty of back-up breast pads with you, and a fresh blouse, even when you aren't with your baby. Actually, especially when you're not with your baby.

So now these same girlfriends owe you a spa day.

You're welcome.

Our first daughter and I couldn't get the nursing thing happening. At first, she wouldn't nurse, and then when she finally decided to nurse, she wanted to eat every hour, hour and a half. My nipples were raw. The kind of raw that made me feel I'd been dragged behind a car facedown with no bra on for fifty miles — that sort of raw. They bled, they oozed, and she screamed. She screamed the bloody house down. So, I stopped. And within a week I was no longer leaking everywhere, and my breasts thanked me. If, for whatever reason, you don't nurse, I'm here to tell you there are some definite upsides to not doing it, and that it's okay.

This is another area where people get super weird and put their beaky noses in your business: the breastfeeding discussion. Here are my thoughts on this, having done both. I nursed my other two daughters with much success, and it was beautiful, and wonderful, and I wouldn't change it for the world. But this notion that you'll bond better with the child you breastfed than the one you didn't is bullshit. Pure, utter bullshit. Making women feel bad about not breastfeeding is just plain wrong. It needs to stop being a thing that breastfeeding women make non-breastfeeding women feel shitty about. I'd like to see someone take that judgmental, backward way of thinking to two men who adopt children, and tell them they just don't love their kids "as deeply" because they didn't nurse them. Or how about two women partners, where maybe one carried the baby and therefore can nurse the child — why not ask the other woman if she just isn't "that connected" to the baby because she isn't the one who's nursing it?

Go ahead, I dare you. Let me know how that goes for you.

Ladies who get all up in other women's business about why they are or aren't breastfeeding need to just stop. Right now, like yesterday. Just shut up. Close your mouth and put your tits away (you know, unless you're nursing at the time, which is *totally fine*!). It's no more your business why another woman is or isn't nursing her child than it's her business if you like to give your husband head or have anal sex.

Awkward, huh? You feel all uncomfortable now, don'tcha?

It's just really none of anyone's damn business what another woman chooses to do with her body or her child. You do what's right for you and your body. You just keep on keeping on, and if you are breastfeeding, that's awesome. And if you're not, that's awesome, too. You are no less a mother, no less loving, and no less a woman for either decision. No one has the right to judge you on this, and if they do, they may not be someone you want to be close with. After all, we're all just trying to do our best out here in this life. So, don't let anyone shame or judge you.

DECIDE ON CHILD-CARE OPTIONS

We all come from different socio-economic backgrounds. One mom, if she lives in Canada, may need to go back to work after the one year of paid leave is up. Another woman might be in the sort of financial situation where she can stay with her baby until she sends them out into the world. Still another mother might be the CEO of a large company, or live in a country or state without any financial parental support, and have to get back in the saddle six weeks after her baby's born. Whatever your PBA (post-baby's arrival) choice or circumstance is, make sure you're set up for success when that day comes by making child-care decisions well in advance.

Will you use a government program or private daycare centre? If so, these fill up super fast, so you might want to get onto multiple waiting lists BBA, as in at conception.

Should you be able to stay home with your baby, do yourself a favour so you don't lose your mind. Join a gym that offers child care. Even if you go for just an hour or two now and then, it'll give you some alone time. It's also some time for your baby to be with other babies and other people. It's great if you can be the one at home taking care of your baby, but that doesn't mean you aren't allowed to keep your life rounded and sane. Join a Mommy and Me group or two — something, anything, to get you out of the house and keep your sanity. If you do happen to join a Mommy and Me walking class, please do all us folks walking the trails a favour. Don't walk side by side with your stroller buddy, or bring your giant baby strollers into teeny-tiny coffee shops. All us parents who have gone before you knew how to share the common walkways and spaces; it would be great if you would do the same. This is another awesome opportunity for you to keep your cool. The cool you had before you were a parent, when you didn't love having to crawl over giant baby strollers to get to the bathroom inside Starbucks. Leave strollers outside and lock them up with bike locks.

The entire city thanks you.

If you're going the private nanny route, I suggest you do yourself and the world another favour: hire a nanny you would love to sit down and have dinner with. You are trusting this person to be a partner in raising your child, so please take the time to find one you really like. Respect. Admire. And would want to be friends with. This person is not just a babysitter while you go out to dinner; they are helping to form your child. You should like them, share some of the same ideals with them, have some similar life opinions, and so on. Find someone who inspires your trust and confidence, and work with them in an honest and respectful way. You are handing them your baby, for God's sake. It's not like they're walking your dog for you.

Whichever PBA route you're going, make sure you do your homework and research the best possible partners to help you raise the most amazing human you can. You were picky when choosing your life partner, so why not be just as picky in deciding on your PBA caregivers.

Your baby thanks you.

Now, all your manual labour is complete, you've done your homework, you've compiled your research, and you're confident in all your choices moving forward. Yay, you! You're doing awesome, you're glowing, you're organized, and now all that's left to do is wait.

Oh yeah, and have sex.

THINGS TO NIBBLE ON

Keep your cool: Take it easy with the social media presence. Decide to give your baby room to breathe, grow, and stand on their own two feet so they can develop a sense of confidence and independence.

Come to a complete agreement on how and where your baby will sleep.

Carefully consider the effects of radiation on your baby, and choose a baby monitor accordingly.

Whether or not you breastfeed is entirely up to you. Don't let anybody sway, judge, or guilt you into going against your own heart.

Know what your PBA plans are for going back to work (or not) and sort out your child-care situation BBA.

And remember to have sex!

Chapter Three

Your Baby Has Arrived, So Now What?

WE'RE DOING IT! We're really blasting through your list of things to do! Isn't this fun? You've committed to, and are holding to, keeping your cool, both with your baby and on all your social media profiles. You and your partner have come to an agreement on where the baby will sleep, and you've done your research on the whole Wi-Fi-radiation-brain-development business. You've decided whether or not you will try to breastfeed. You know just how long you'll be staying home with your new family member, and you've arranged for child care as needed. I'm pretty sure you're having sex, too.

This is going to be a super-short chapter, because I'm not psychic, so I have no idea what sort of baby you're going to have, or what the energy of your current living situation is like. So, with this in mind, I'm just going to hit you with the for-sure things you'll want to keep in mind PBA.

By this point you've either successfully pushed a tiny human out of your body, or are recovering from your C-section. You might be at the hospital, or maybe you have just brought home your bundle of joy after the adoption process or watching your surrogate deliver your child. Whatever way your new family member came into the world, the outcome is the same for each and every one of you. You now have this teeny-tiny human being who relies solely on you for everything, and let's be honest — you're probably more than a little freaked out about this.

And that's okay.

GETTING TO KNOW YOUR BABY

The cool thing about this new little person living in your house is that they have absolutely no idea that *you* have no idea what you're doing. They also have no expectations, as they have no clue what to expect. Cool, right? I mean, if there are no expectations set upon you by this tiny person, then how can you let them down?

Other than the obvious: you could not feed them enough, not change them in a timely fashion, not keep them warm or cool. But I mean, who's going let those things slide? Not you. You know why you aren't going to forget any of those things?

Because your baby won't let you.

If they're hungry, man oh man, you will know.

If their diaper is too wet, you will know that, too.

If they're cold, they will sound and look it.

How?

Because most babies will cry to alert you to their needs. If your new family member is like our eldest, your baby will have a very powerful set of lungs with which to express their discomfort loudly and clearly. If, on the other hand, you have one who's a little more chill than that, more like our middle daughter, they might just grumble and fuss to let you know that something isn't right. If you have this sort of baby, you'll need to do a little more guesswork. That can seem scary, but let me tell you this: if you have a super-chill baby, they will give you a fair bit of time before their grumbling turns into full-blown "will you please do something, Mom, Dad; I am *uncomfortable here.*" So you'll have some time to work it out.

The other amazing thing about babies is that they really do have different cries for their various discomforts. Our youngest had very clear and distinct cries for everything, which helped to remove the guesswork. In no time, you will come to decipher what each cry represents, and you'll be that cool parent, when your friends are over and your baby cries, who says, "Oh, Baby's diaper is full of poop." Then, in front of your friends you'll open up your baby's diaper and *voilà* — it will in fact be filled to the brim. You'll smile a cool *I've got this* smile and your friends will nod their admiration for you and your mad parenting skills, while holding their noses.

Keep in mind that all babies are different — they are as unique as we full-grown babies are. No two are alike, which is why you can't just follow along with any book that tells you exactly what your baby will do at every stage of development. You need to listen to your baby, and you need to be patient. Maybe your baby doesn't get their first tooth until they're eight months old. Or perhaps they don't crawl until they're a year, but your book and the twelve apps you downloaded say they should have been on hands and knees by the time they were four months old.

Relax.

If your doctor tells you your baby is healthy and you know it in your heart, just relax and let them do their thing. It's all good. I've never seen a university student trucking across campus on their hands and knees.

Relax. Keep your cool. If you're told everything is okay, try to believe it!

You don't know what you're going to end up with until your baby is home for a few weeks. Once you're all settled into your new life and routine, you will come to deeply understand your baby. If within days of being home, you're pretty sure you've popped out an incredibly fussy baby, don't wait to get help — seek it early on, for the sake of your own sanity and the comfort of your baby. Yannick and I fumbled around blindly on our own for so long, desperately trying to guess what was wrong with our eldest daughter. There were plenty of tears from her, and from us. We felt so helpless. We watched her screaming out, clearly in agony, never able to get comfortable enough to sleep more than a couple of hours at a time. We felt defeated. Looking back now, I wish I had done more than just hang on for dear life and "wait for the moment to pass." But we didn't know any differently. We had no friends who had children, there was no internet at the time, and those who had gone before us weren't any more educated than we were about babies who were so uncomfortable. We gave her gripe water, we massaged her belly, and sometimes we just let her cry herself back to sleep. It was a difficult time, one I wouldn't want to repeat, for her sake or ours. We were committed to doing the best we could with what we had, and that was what we did. Today, Brianna suffers from many food allergies, so on the one hand, at least we know most of what she went through had nothing to do with what we were or weren't doing properly. Thirty-one years ago, no one was really educated about food allergies in the way we are now. Her situation was out of our control. We had no idea what the problem was and no direction as to what to do.

One thing I recommend is to keep visitors, and busyness, down to a dull roar in the first few weeks. It is incredibly exciting to have this new human in your life, and most everybody close to you will want to come see, hold, and meet the baby. But in order for you to have some serious, quiet bonding time, I

> Keep visitors and busyness down to a dull roar in the first few weeks.

strongly suggest allowing only your "ride-or-die" peeps for the first few weeks. Just because we're used to a world that moves at warp speed, in which we keep ourselves stimulated 24/7, doesn't mean your baby wants that lifestyle, too. They've just arrived from the most beautiful place of warmth, safety, and what I like to call "muffled silence"; let's not blow their minds within the first few weeks of their arrival by bombarding them with stimulus. Okay?

By now you might be thinking, "Wow, Shantelle's such a ray of sunshine, spreading good news and cheer everywhere she goes." I told you from the get-go that I was going to be frank with you. I'm not here to freak you out. I'm here to share with you that no matter how easy or hard a delivery, no matter how happy or fussy a baby you have, the power they have over your life is up to you. If you throw your hands up in the air and give in to defeat or your hormonally imbalanced state at the first sign of difficulty, I have news for you — it is going to be a long eighteen years. Like, *really long*. The most important thing about being a parent is being humble. Nobody has to go it alone.

LET OTHERS HELP AS MUCH AS THEY CAN

There are so many resources out there these days, there's no need to try to be a superhuman. You're incredibly blessed to be a parent in this day and age. Take *full* advantage of all of it.

Help may come in the form of your mom moving in temporarily (as mine did). I hate to freak out the partners who are reading along with you, but having a family member come stay with you can be incredibly helpful and comforting. My mom moved in for a couple of weeks every time I delivered one of our girls. With Dominique, my husband was in New Zealand for the month before her birth and for the first three weeks of her life. So, my mom came and helped me for two months. She even let me fly her all the way to L.A. to stay with me for a couple of weeks when Mikaela, our youngest, was born in a city I had lived in for only two months. I had just one good girlfriend there at the time, and she was busy with her two little boys. I knew how busy her life was, because mine was, too. Wherever you are geographically, or emotionally, in the world, whether you're close to your mom, or your partner's mom, or your sister or your brother-in-law, if there's any way to have somebody come stay, do it. Especially if you're the sort of person who overwhelms easily, like me. That extra pair of hands and the wisdom of their having "been there, done that" will give you confidence until you can find your own. If the people close to you can't come and stay, see if they can each commit to bringing you a day or two of premade meals. Or ask if they'll take shifts hanging around for a couple of hours so you can nap or, you know, shower, or run the errands you used to dislike but now would give just about anything for, just to get some fresh air and be all on your own. Anything, really, that can help take a little bit of the load off you while you adjust and settle in to being responsible for this very small stranger living in your home.

> If the people close to you can't come and stay, see if they can each commit to bringing you a day or two of premade meals.

So, you're being supported by family/friends, and we have you back home. Your little bundle of human joy has moved in with you, and, if you carried the baby yourself, you're beginning to go through the bowling-ball-boob thing as your milk really comes in. It's not the best feeling in the world. And if you delivered vaginally, then sitting, standing, going to the bathroom — everything — is uncomfortable. I haven't had a C-section, but from what I've gleaned from my friends who have, I understand that your vag is happy, but standing straight up and holding your newborn are both incredibly difficult after surgery. No matter which way your baby made its great escape from your uterus and entered the world, either way is pretty brutal, and sucks.

But here's the good news: nothing lasts forever. And if it were really so unbelievably scarring, horrific, and unforgettable, people — myself included — wouldn't go back for more. So "nothing lasts forever" couldn't be a more appropriate mantra during these days. In fact, the whole time will become a blur. You won't even remember what any of it felt like within weeks, I kid you not. Like, not at all. And your vag will still work. If you're lucky, like I was, it'll be up and running long before the six weeks your doctor suggested. You'll be back to having sex once again, just like I've been telling you to do.

It really is all good news here, ladies.

I do want to encourage you to really follow the at-home healing instructions of your birthing advisers. Do whatever they tell you to because they've delivered more babies than you have, they know what they're talking about, and they have your comfort, and the comfort of your baby, in mind. Did I mention you need to find a doctor or practitioner whom you trust and can talk to about anything? Oh yeah, and if your parts are working and you're feeling amorous, do yourself a favour and use birth control. You *can* get pregnant when breastfeeding. Just ask my friend who found out she was pregnant when her baby was four months old. Yes. Pregnant again, after just giving birth *four months before*. Wrap it up, men. It's the least you could do for her.

BE MENTALLY PREPARED: ANYTHING CAN HAPPEN

I can't really advise you on the rest of what may or may not happen because, like I said, I don't know what kind of baby you're going to end up with. Will your first be the dream sleeping baby I was blessed with when I had my second, or will you get a more challenging tiny human right out of the gate, like I did with daughter number one? Nobody knows. And chances are you won't either for the first few days — maybe even longer. This is the thing about babies. They're teeny-tiny mysteries that don't come with a handbook, and no matter how many books you've read, none of them will reveal your baby's mysterious ways. Reading can give you glimpses into what to expect when your newborn comes home — the sort of universal things of childbirth and newborns — but your baby is unique to you, your genetics, your environment, and so on.

It really is a guessing game for the first couple of months. The best thing I can tell you about bringing your baby home is that you should be prepared for anything and everything to happen.

Even small things. For example, when you're changing your son, there's a pretty high probability that he will pee into the air, and all over you, and even into his own face when the cold air hits his penis. Make sure to have an extra cloth nearby to place over him while you change him. (How would you know this if you'd never seen it?) I have seen sons of family members and girlfriends do this, and it is really funny, but probably not at 2 a.m., when you have both eyes in one socket thanks to exhaustion.

At every step of the way, keep reminding yourself that this is a giant life adjustment. It's going to take time to get used to this stranger living in your home, so be patient. Be patient with yourself, your partner, and your baby; this is all new to all of you. Give yourself time to figure it all out. Remember what it was like when you first started dating your spouse? I'm sure there were all sorts of guffaws, hiccups, misunderstandings, and WTF moments. But look at you now — you've made it. You're under the same roof, a healthy, functioning couple who are building not only a life but a family together. If you were able to get through all that you didn't know about each other and still end up in this place of utopia, then why wouldn't starting a relationship with your baby be the same? Getting to know one another, to understand your baby's cries, their body language, and their needs will take time. You need to remember to be patient and to be kind to yourself, your partner, and — I'll say this even though it's obvious — also to your baby.

> It's going to take time to get used to this stranger living in your home, so be patient.

OVERWHELMED? SEEK HELP RIGHT AWAY

The most important thing you can do is recognize that you feel freaked out. At the first sign of feeling overwhelmed, lost, or "not right," stop and ask for help. Don't hesitate and don't feel bad about it. If your new human friend is on the more challenging side of the baby spectrum, please do yourselves both a favour and get help right away. Exhaustion and frustration can easily take over sanity. I know what it's like to be so overwhelmed, to be so completely exhausted, that you feel as though you're physically living outside your body, and to get to a dark place where you're tempted to shake your baby to get it to stop screaming. That is not the solution.

Never.

Ever.

As I've said, our eldest was an incredibly challenging baby. There were days and nights when she would scream for hours, and hours, and hours. Walls and doors were punched by my husband, and hundreds of kilometres were driven, because that was one of the only things that soothed her — the driving, obviously, *not* the punching. I cannot even begin to tell you how many tears I shed. I was scared. Overwhelmed. Frustrated and exhausted. When I found myself at the end of my rope, I threw things, I cried in her face, I begged her to stop screaming, to just go to sleep. Just typing these words brings those feelings of utter failure back to me, as if they happened just yesterday. It was rough then, and it's rough living with it still. Lucky for me, I lived close to my mother. She was instrumental in helping the three of us, our little family, pull through it. But it was not easy, and we could not have managed it alone. Don't ever tell yourself that you need to go it alone, or that if you were a good mother, your baby wouldn't be crying. Don't be ashamed or feel guilty about asking for help. When you're drowning and someone puts out their hand to pull you up, grab it. Don't wait until you're sinking; ask for help the moment your head touches water.

That's why earlier, I said it was so important to get an amazing doctor, practitioner, midwife, or doula whom you trust with your entire soul. If you choose wisely, this person will be the one to walk you through the harder, darker times you may experience in the beginning of your relationship with your baby. No matter what, you can't do it alone, especially if you end up with a challenging infant.

So, promise me this: you will get help, and you will do it sooner rather than later.

Taking this topic one step further, let's briefly discuss postpartum depression. I was fortunate not to suffer from it, so I won't speak too much on the matter, other than to say that I cannot stress how crucial it is to be humble and in tune with yourself. You know yourself better than anybody, and only you will know if you mentally don't feel like yourself. Something as routine and standard as a colicky baby can send new moms over the edge. Getting help isn't a sign of weakness; it's the exact opposite! It shows great strength and tremendous humility. (And hello, new parents, trust me when I tell you this: humility is something you should get used to having, now that you have a child. You will need to be humble a great deal during the journey you are now on; ego has no place in child-rearing.) Should you have the faintest

Getting help isn't a sign of weakness; it's the exact opposite!

inkling that things aren't going well, that your thoughts don't make sense, that you're sinking into despair, then please reach out to that amazing practitioner you brought on to care for you, and let them do just that: care for you.

There is no shame in not being able to do this alone.

There is no shame in feeling overwhelmed.

There is no shame in feeling like you're in over your head.

You don't get in your car to go on a cross-country road trip without a GPS, and you wouldn't make a world-famous chef's dish without using their recipe. So why would you try to bring home, and deal with, a newborn baby without any help?

You might need a lot of help; you might need only a little.

And that's okay.

So, partners who are reading this together, make this vow, out loud — even record it on your phones: "We promise to watch over one another, to ensure each of us is receiving the support they need during the first few months, and if one of us needs more support than the other can provide, we vow to make sure to go and get it."

And then you know, if everything is all healed up, and you get the urge …

Have sex!

THINGS TO NIBBLE ON

No two humans are alike, and the same goes for babies. Give yourself the time to get to know yours.

Don't be afraid to let others help. It seriously takes a village, so pull in all the reinforcements you have access to.

Be mentally and physically prepared for the fact that anything can, and will, happen. Like any new relationship, this will be filled with unknowns, so don't expect to have it all worked out in the blink of an eye.

If you feel frightened and not yourself, don't bury it; talk to your doctor. If you're struggling, and especially if you feel like you might cause harm to the baby or yourself, seek help. Immediately.

Keep having sex.

Chapter Four

The Shit *Will* Hit the Fan

THE COOL THING ABOUT being organized is that it minimizes the chaos in your life. Order also has an extremely calming effect on our spirit, which is why I'm going to harp on it throughout this book. I want you to be able to relax into your new life with your baby, instead of worrying about where your breast pads are.

Now that the baby's home, you're taking the time to get to know them. You've recognized that you're not supermom, and so you're letting people help, asking Mom or someone else close to stay a while if at all possible, or at least to visit regularly. You're mentally prepared for the fact that the unexpected will happen. And you're keeping a close eye on yourself and your partner for any signs of being overwhelmed or in despair, and getting help *immediately* if anything crops up.

Now let's move on to the good stuff.

LIFE IS GOING TO GET REAL CRAZY
FROM TIME TO TIME

And that's okay.

The shit will hit the fan at different stages for every-body. As I've mentioned, our first daughter was a challenge the minute we brought her home. What I haven't shared with you — and is in fact the best part of this story — is that shortly after delivery, as in hours, Brianna latched nicely onto my breast. My doctor came in to check on us. Keep in mind, this was 1989, and I had chosen a doctor who had a lovely bedside manner and delivered babies at the newest, most state-of-the-art hospital that Toronto had at the time. He was bringing babies into a world where labour and delivery happened in what looked like a swanky hotel room, and because I was scared shitless, that alone was good enough for me. Delivering there was the best decision I had made in my young life, right after picking Yannick as a life partner. It was seriously a joy; the nurses were divine, happy, and excited to be working in such a tranquil place, bringing new tiny humans into our big, beautiful world. In fact, if I had wanted to, had I known more about child-birth, I could have had a midwife or a doula with me, and had a water birth! It was the epitome of chill. And delivery was, I'm sorry to brag, pretty easy, too. At least, once they put me on the necessary Pitocin drip to induce me, because my water had broken, but Brianna was so comfy in there she didn't want to come out. Once your water breaks, the clock is ticking. Brianna needed to get out of there as my amniotic fluid was gone! Thanks to the above-mentioned "drip," which encourages your body to help the baby vacate the building quickly, I delivered her within six hours.

You see, my body really likes to get pregnant fast and furious, but it doesn't feel quite the same way about delivering the babies to the world. So until I was induced, my labour was super slow. I would dilate little by little, until *bam*! All of a sudden, within a couple of hours, I would go from "hey, can you bring me a burger?" to squeezing Yannick's arms with a death grip while doing my best "hoo hoo hahh" breathing. Even if I'd wanted an epidural, by the time it fully kicked in, I would have already delivered the baby. So, ladies who are adamant about getting the epidural, just be mindful that you can miss your window of opportunity. Now, had I had to labour longer than six hours, I'm not quite sure I would be sitting here telling the story so happily. Don't hate me, but I also needed no stitches — as in zero, zilch, nada. Yannick likes to take all the credit for that because he happily performed the vaginal "stretching exercises" our Lamaze teacher encouraged us to do. And my kids thankfully had lovely, tiny skulls. (Such considerate daughters from the get-go!) It was a good time. So good that I let them send me home when Brianna was thirty-six hours old, because *hello, I had this!* In fact, even my doctor who came in the next morning to check on me thought we were amazing, that we were naturals at the breastfeeding game, the sleeping game, all of it. He even went so far as to lean over Brianna, stroke her teeny-tiny head, and declare, "This is the happiest, most contented baby I've ever delivered. You will have such an easy time with her. Congratulations."

And that, my friends, is how my GP cursed me and my beautiful newborn daughter.

I believe wholeheartedly that it was right then and there that he reversed our fortune. As much as we had *had it* in the hospital hours before we were discharged, it became an entirely different scene the moment we got home.

When we got home, our shit hit the fan *immediately*, and it became really clear, really fast that I, we, did *not have it*. At all.

I had no milk, I had no patience, and I had no fucking clue.

I was way out of my league. She was a difficult baby, because as we now know, she suffered with many allergies. Back in a day when there weren't a lot of non-wheat, non-dairy, non-soy options — not that we knew that was what she needed, anyway — this was challenging, to say the least. She suffered for months because we just didn't know what was wrong with her; even our GP was stumped. Bless his heart, but he wasn't the sort of guy who was going to send us to somebody who would know. It just wasn't his way. We were too young, too battle weary to even think to ask, and it wasn't like we could go online to research alternative care for her, because in 1989 there was no internet.

How is that for a WTF moment for you?

I know that some of you don't know life *without* the internet. But that resource is very, very recent in the evolution of human events and babies. When we brought our beautiful first-born daughter home, we were completely alone, young, and lost. My heart still aches as I write about Brianna's first six months of life. It didn't get easier until her teeth started to come in and she needed less and less baby formula, being able to eat more "adult food" on her own. Life got easier for all of us when that happened. But eating adult food still didn't help much with her sleep. In fact, at thirty-one, she still doesn't sleep well. Poor girl.

The temperament of your new little person will have a lot to do with your shit hitting the fan. For Yannick and me, man oh man, did we have some knock-down, drag-out fights in those first few months. Remember when I told you about the fists in the walls and doors? Well, not all of them were thanks to Brianna screaming at the top of her lungs, or not sleeping or eating. Some had to do with the fact that we were incredibly tired, stressed-out, young, and overwhelmed. Maybe you're totally prepared because you have been planning on having your baby for five, ten, fifteen, or twenty years. Congratulations, that's awesome. But it doesn't always work out that way. The whole mothering thing was sprung on me; it hadn't really occurred to me that I would have children. Yet here I am, three young women later, and I honestly have never done anything quite as rewarding, or challenging. So, no matter what your plans or intentions are, there is a high probability that at some point, the shit is going to hit the fan, meaning things are going to get so overwhelming and intense that you or your partner, or both, are going to lose it. You might as well be prepared.

How do you prepare for something you don't know is coming? It won't be the same for everybody. For some of you, it might not be that intense — not everyone is going to need to ram their fist into a wall — and you might even doubt that it's coming at all. But let me assure you, whether you have a mild case of shit-fan-hitting, or yours is more of a "we can't even see the fan because of all the shit that is hitting it," I can assure you that on some level it is *coming for you.*

You may still doubt that I know what I'm talking about, because hey, I don't know you, I don't know your partner. Maybe neither of you are wall-punching, door-busting sort of folk. Well, okay, you may very well *not* have those tendencies at all, BBA. BBA, you might even argue respectfully, never raising your voices, letting the other person finish their thought, ensuring their statement is complete before you respond. You may be the best conflict-resolving couple on the entire planet, BBA. But I am here to tell you that we weren't the door-busting, wall-punching sort of fighters, either. We didn't get like that until we had gone *weeks* without a full night's sleep, combined with feeling so out of our depth that we questioned whether we were good at anything at all.

Having a baby changes a person.

> Having a baby changes a person.

Don't expect to have anything go the way it used to in your relationship. Unlike your best girlfriends who have already gone down this road but didn't share any truths with you, I'm here to tell you that parenting is like nothing you've ever done. It is all new. *You* are all new, so be ready for some serious change. Just like in *Game of Thrones*, "Winter is coming." Trust me, from my experience, shit is going to fly.

You might be reading this, saying, "Shit, Sunshine Shantelle, at it again with a whole lot of uplifting, encouraging advice. I kinda hate this." To that, I say *good.* I'm glad it's upsetting you. You know why? The truth is sometimes difficult to swallow, but wouldn't you rather go into this new *lifetime* venture having all the facts? True facts, even if they're ugly. I know I would.

Remember what I said in the Introduction, about how it's going to be war? You don't go into a war wearing rose-coloured glasses, carrying only a flask of water and a white flag. No. You go in prepared, because you want to come out of it alive. Parenting is the same. You want to raise your new human to be an amazing one — one that you even want to spend all your time with. I'm on your side. I want you to end up with strong, fantastic relationships, not only with your children, but with your partner as well. Perhaps most importantly with your partner because, hey, when the kids are gone, that's who you'll be left with.

The truth is I want you to have it all, because you can. It's going to take a huge commitment from you, and a great deal of work, but I believe you can do this.

Something else I want to bring up here, while we're on the difficult subject of truth. The truth is I want you to succeed. The truth is I wish I had known then what I know now. Isn't that always the way of life? Twenty-twenty hindsight? Parenting is the toughest job you will ever have in your life, but it is also the most fulfilling, most rewarding one. If you do it right. If parented right, your children will grow up to be your favourite people in the world. You will drop any and all plans should one of your kids contact you and invite you out instead. This will be your reward for putting in the hard work right from the beginning. Yay, you!

Now that we know there will inevitably be challenges, how should you cope when the parenting or relationship train is going off the rails? For me, back then and even now, I find the best thing to do when I'm feeling overwhelmed is leave the room. To go catch my breath, be quiet and alone until I feel the upset slip away. Instinctively, I know this best, and I run hot, so I don't always react calmly. It's not my tendency to bite my tongue, which is why it's so important (incase you're like me) to have a place to retreat to.

HAVE YOUR OWN SPACE TO RETREAT TO

This is important to plan BBA. You and your partner must determine where your "quiet" zone will be when the shit hits the fan. For example, if Yannick and I were having kids today, he would pick his garage. That would be his go-to spot, for sure. I would most likely pick my back garden, where I have a manmade waterfall that runs over rocks, making the most calming sound, and nature close at hand.

> You need to have an escape route, somewhere to go to when it all gets to be too much.

Definite nerve-soothers for me. Get in touch with what calms you, what allows you to stop, regroup, and hit reset. When it all gets to be too much, it's essential to be able to gather yourself, centre yourself, take some deep breaths and calm down. It may happen to both parents at the same time because your baby is in agony from teething. It may come about because you each thought the other was handling dinner, only to discover nobody planned dinner at all. And so on. Whatever the cause of the upset, the bottom line is you need to have an escape route, somewhere to go to when it all gets to be too much.

If your baby is fussing and you both just need a break, put them in a comfortable place in the crib and step back. I don't know of any baby dying from crying alone for ten or fifteen minutes. Go and get yourself right. Take the time to settle down — your baby will thank you. Babies only know energy, so make sure yours is all good when you're dealing with a cranky newborn.

FIGURE OUT HOW TO CALM YOUR BABY

When the baby first comes home, this might prove a difficult task. Trying to calm a newborn can be like attempting to put a jigsaw puzzle together without the photo. To make matters worse, this puzzle has lungs, and it screams at you when you put the wrong piece in the wrong spot. But once you figure it out, it can work like magic.

We discovered pretty early on that when Brianna got overtired, or if her stomach was bothering her, the only thing that brought her any sort of comfort was to be loaded into the car and taken for a drive. Sometimes, if we hadn't fought during her hours of upset, we would both take her. If we hadn't managed to keep our own tempers in check, one would stay home, regrouping, while the other enjoyed some quiet time to themselves in the car. Driving won't necessarily be the thing that brings your baby back from the brink of a tiny-human meltdown, but whatever it is, try to figure it out early on. It will save you from many meltdowns of your own.

Maybe a nice, warm, candlelit bath *with* you can do double duty, calming both you and your baby down.

Maybe you can give your baby an ice-cold washcloth that's been in the freezer for days to gnaw on, soothing sore gums.

And here's a thing that can be surprising: your baby might just need to be left alone. They could be overstimulated and just want to be in their own space so they can fall asleep. Sometimes a baby will cry and cry, and then you put them down just to figure out what's going on, and presto! The baby calms down. Just like you, sometimes even a baby just wants to be left alone.

Try everything until you hit the jackpot. By now you'll be pretty attuned to your little person, so you'll know which cry or scream represents which ailment and you'll be able to act accordingly.

You might be saying, "How can I think about what's going to calm my baby down during a meltdown if they aren't even here yet?" This fear may make you anxious or panicked, making you doubt yourself before you're even in that place. But guess what? It's your baby. You will know what to do; you will figure it out. Because the alternative is to just stand there while your baby freaks out and screams for hours and you cry back at them. And you know what? That might happen, too. It happened to me a few times. Actually, who am I kidding — it was more than a "few times." It was lots and lots and *lots* of times, if I'm being totally transparent with you, as all good friends should be. Right? Yeah, I'm putting all those "friends" who didn't tell you about your sandpaper vag and your bowling-ball breasts on blast.

Anyway, carrying on.

One night, when Yannick was filming a series in L.A., Mikaela, our youngest, was screaming her baby head off in our bed. I couldn't get her to nurse, and there was nothing I could do to soothe her. She was my *third* baby. None of the tricks I had collected over the years of being a mom were working. I paced back and forth with her for what seemed like half the night. Finally, I couldn't do it anymore. I held her at arm's length and cried right along with her. I looked her in her little blue eyes and cried. Then I laid her on the floor in our big walk-in closet (and when I say "closet," it was actually a bedroom that had been converted into a closet, so calm down, everybody, it's not like I put her in a 2 x 6 closet with mirrored sliding doors) while I went and grabbed her bassinette. I wheeled the cradle into the closet, kissed her little face, our tears running into one another's, and tucked her in, turned off the light, closed the door and left her there. I lay in my bed and cried until she stopped crying, and then finally I went to sleep.

> As a parent of a newborn, you will have successes and defeats, but neither will define you.

As a parent of a newborn, you will have successes and defeats, but neither will define you. Just get back up and keep going. Eventually, you'll become one of those cool moms who can say to a friend, "He does this all the time, believe me. He'll be asleep within five minutes." You will become a soothing and knowing-your-baby guru in no time.

And I know I'm like a broken record on this topic, but that's because it is incredibly important — in fact, it might even be the *most important* piece of the new-parent puzzle: as I said in Chapter Three, if you're not getting to the bottom of what ails your baby, get help. Don't hesitate, don't feel guilty, don't feel embarrassed. Remember that it takes a village, so embrace all the help you can get. There's zero shame in it. Believe me when I tell you that moments like mine with the closet should not be the norm for you. If they are, *get help*.

Please don't allow any of this to put panic into your heart. Pretty early on, you will find out how to soothe your child. Trust me on this. Have I lied to you yet?

You know what the outcome was of that night in 1996 that I put Mikaela in the closet? I lived, and she lived. We made it through that night, and you, too, will make it through all of yours.

Now that we're clear and confident about all that, let's talk about the art of fighting with your partner — or rather, of making up after a fight. This was hard for me to learn, but when I really grasped the concept, it not only improved my marriage but also trickled into every other aspect of my life.

BE THE FIRST TO SAY YOU'RE SORRY

I actually really like this helpful little tidbit about what to do when the shit hits the fan, because it manages to completely defuse the situation every single time. It will also come in real handy as your newborn becomes a moving object and you overreact at them for spilling grape juice on your brand-new couch. (Which will totally happen, so get ready for it. If you want to avoid it because you own a ton of really expensive shit, don't give them grape juice. Or just give them the clear grape juice, which freaks me out, because it's not purple like grapes. That seems odd. Unless, of course, it is made from green grapes, which is entirely possible ... Sorry, I digress. Let's get back on point.)

Thirty-two years with my husband have taught me a great many things about myself, and one of them is to take ownership when I'm wrong. Whatever your relationship balance is, whether you're the natural pain in the ass in your relationship or your partner is, it never hurts to apologize first for your part in things.

> True humility is saying you're sorry for your part of the shit hitting the fan, even when you didn't start it.

This was super difficult for me to learn. Like, nearly fucking impossible. I was like a vampire in the sunlight when I initially began to work on this. True humility is saying you're sorry for your part of the shit hitting the fan, even when you didn't start it. Taking ownership for your part even when your partner is still sulking over in the corner and giving you the cold pouty shoulder, and not in the cute sexy-lingerie-model way.

Listen, we're all assholes, and we're all wrong, a lot of the time. The sooner you come to terms with that and learn to say you're sorry, the smoother your parenting will be, and the healthier your relationship with your significant other. And, although I love this philosophy and totally subscribe to it as an amazing way to live, I still find it incredibly difficult to execute. Why? Because

I'm a giant pain in the ass. Which means I'm often at the centre of the shitstorm in my house.

But after all these years, I'm pretty good at apologizing. Try it, you might like it, because it also makes it super easy to then …

Have sex!

THINGS TO NIBBLE ON

Life is going to be totally crazy from time to time; this is normal and to be expected. Take it easy, breathe, and relax. Just because it's not going perfectly doesn't mean it isn't going well.

Ensure that you have a way to retreat to your own space. Set up a spot in your home — your happy place — where you can each retreat and calm down in the face of overwhelming stress.

Figure out how to calm your baby. It'll take time, it'll take some trial and error, but you'll figure it out.

Be humble — meaning be the first to say you're sorry. This might be really hard for you to swallow (it was for me). But once I got in the habit of it, it made all the difference.

Chapter Five

Let's Talk About Sex!

THIS IS WHEN WE'RE GOING to start to have some fun! You now fully understand and have the incredibly real expectation that the shit is going to hit the fan at some point during the adjustment period of your new life. You'll ensure that you know, going into PBA, there will be times when you just need to be alone and regroup. You're prepared to collect the tools you need to soothe your newborn more easily, knowing that it doesn't mean certain death if your little friend cries for a little while, unattended but in a safe place (and also knowing that over time, you *will* gain confidence). You've embraced the fact that you're not right all the time, and you don't mind being the first person to apologize after a fight.

And once you get good at saying sorry, and being sorry, you're going to want to have sex, so how perfect is it that this is our next topic?

Yay! Lucky us!

BE PATIENT WITH YOUR
BODY'S RECOVERY

One of my girlfriends was recently pregnant with her first baby. A few of us were talking with her about (here it comes) her vag and what it might be like post-baby, and one friend said, "It will never be the same, but that's not all bad."

My response was a little different. I simply said, "Well, I've had no complaints." We all laughed. At least, those of us on the other side of it — with still happy, healthy, orgasm-producing bits — laughed. Our pregnant friend gave a nervous chuckle.

Let's talk briefly about this new trend of vaginal rejuvenation surgery that women are *actually getting*. I want to know: is it really necessary? I mean, honestly, ladies, is it? Aren't you all being just a tad paranoid? And, if I may be frank, a bit *extra*? I've been with my husband since we were teenagers, and let me tell you that my husband's bits aren't exactly the same as they were when he was nineteen now that he's fifty. And I don't find him any less sexy than I did when he was nineteen. Actually, all our years together and all the storms we've endured have made him even sexier to me. Go figure.

Don't get caught up, or hung up, on the optics of life. Be present in the *now* of life. But if you are that girl who feels the need to get her vag tightened up after she's all done pushing out her kids, have at it. Live and let live, I always say! If you've read my blog on shantellebisson.com, you know that I'm totally pro plastic surgery, so go for it, ladies, if that's what tickles you and your partner's fancy. I just think it's important for you to know that it isn't necessary; you shouldn't feel as though you must do it to ensure your partner's pleasure. Believe me, it comes back! I mean, three kids later and I have had zero complaints from my smoking-hot husband about the condition of my vag.

There is also the unrealistic expectation to look like you didn't just have a baby as soon as you push that baby out. I don't know what's with the dialogue out there in the world. Why do so many magazines insist on telling women how this celebrity or that celebrity is back into her skinny jeans in *four weeks*, or is even thinner, just two months after giving birth, than she was before?

> There is the unrealistic expectation to look like you didn't just have a baby as soon as you push that baby out.

This is where I'm going to need you and your baby-making cohort to slow down and keep some things in perspective. You don't have a personal chef, day nanny, night nanny, personal trainer, or personal assistant doing anything and everything for you, do you? So that all you have to do is eat your perfectly pH-balanced, chef-prepared meals while you work out four hours a day, and your daytime nanny feeds the baby a bottle of your breast milk?

You probably also didn't do what's called the Manhattan Delivery, where you go in for a scheduled C-section about two to four weeks out from your delivery date so your baby doesn't have that final, and usually largest, growth spurt, which stretches your skin the most (and which is often when the worst stretch marks and most weight gain tend to happen). I'm here to tell you that's insane. I cannot even deal with discussing it. It's wrong on so many fucking levels, that even for me, a person who works extremely hard at not judging others for their life choices, this is just one thing I can't get behind. This behaviour I judge, and I judge harshly. You would really take away your child's right to fully develop so you can avoid weight gain and stretch marks? Wow. Wow. Just *wow*. The doctors who perform these procedures should be ashamed of themselves. God only knows what long-term side effects these children will have because of this narcissistic practice. It should just *stop*.

But I know you are not like that. You wouldn't dream of pulling your baby out of your body prematurely for your own vanity. Because you won't do that, I trust you will do your best to manage your weight in a healthy manner, to the benefit of both yourself and your baby. If you're not that super-lucky, super-privileged, one-in-a-million mom who can afford all those extra hands and help, that's okay. Most of us aren't. You are you. You will heal when you heal. You will lose the weight when you lose it. You're not living your life poorly, right? You're making healthy food choices, and you're getting in exercise when and how you can. You are doing your best, and that's the most you can do. Even though I put on double the average amount of weight with each pregnancy, I managed to lose every last pound of it, eventually. So, don't stress, just keep your eye on the prize, and enjoy your baby.

Getting back to the state of your vag, post-delivery: If your partner *loves* you, and *cherishes* you, and *honours* you, then if your vag is that little bit looser because you welcomed their incredible son or daughter (or more than one) into the world through it, I don't think you're going to have any complaints.

You gave them offspring. Girl. *Relax*. Relish it.

You participated in a *miracle*. You are blessed, and you are *lucky*. Not all women who desire to give life to a child have that blessing, so stop getting hung up on the teeny-tiny, insignificant details.

> Not all women who desire to give life to a child have that blessing, so stop getting hung up on the insignificant details.

WHEN WILL I BE READY TO HAVE SEX?

To those of you who were fortunate enough to adopt your beautiful child or use a surrogate, then you can skip right over the gory details of this part, because it deals with "when will my lady bits be usable again," and as yours were never in play, you're good to go. For those who had C-sections, you might need to wait at least four or even six weeks until your postpartum follow-up. This is when your sutures are removed, if your doctor didn't use dissolvable ones. By that point, you should start to feel like your ab muscles are in a place where they can allow you to not just lie there and take it. But I would definitely check with your doctor on that. A C-section is major surgery, and you need to recover from it before you get back in the saddle! Although honestly, you did just carry and give life to your partner's child, so maybe you deserve a few missionary-style orgasms for a little while. In fact, all of you in this category with no healing to wait for could go ahead and have sex right now while the rest of the class reads this next part of the book.

The next most frequently asked question is "Do I really need to wait six weeks?" For most of us in a healthy relationship, six weeks is like waiting through the Ice Age. It sounds, and feels, like *forever*. To be brutally honest with you, I'd say it all depends on your pain threshold.

If I can take you all back to that time — or maybe more than one time, if you're like me — that you put a tampon in and then tried to pull it out immediately because it wasn't sitting in the right spot. Remember how it felt all scrapy, and dry, and uncomfortable? Well, now imagine that feeling *on crack*! Then multiply it by, like, a thousand.

When you pee, it burns. It feels like dragging sandpaper across your dry skin, then pouring rubbing alcohol on it. Here's an exercise that can give your partner a sense of it: Go get the roughest sandpaper you can find at your local Home Depot and rub your lover's calf with it, a lot. Make sure that you break the skin, making a ton of tiny little scratches. Then take some rubbing alcohol, in high concentration, and just pour a steady stream of it up and down their calf, counting as high as you think a good, long morning pee would take you, then stop. If you do this little couple's experiment, then and only then will your partner have the faintest idea of the pain in your vag after you've pushed a human being out of it. If your partner won't do this homework assignment with you, I'd seriously question their commitment to understanding you, and to their willingness to walk a mile in your shoes or see life through your eyes.

I kid, I kid. They totally love you. I'm sure of it.

Now back to you. When you sit, it hurts. I'm sure all your "friends" who went before you into baby-making land didn't tell you this. Ladies, it seriously hurts like hell. I mean, childbirth itself has an end in sight: eight, twelve, twenty-four, *maybe* forty-eight hours, and you're through it. But this vag pain … it seriously feels like it's just going to go on, and on, and on. Each day that it still fucking hurts, you're absolutely going to want to remove that entire section of your body.

> You're going to feel as though your pieces will never be the same.

But I have good news for you. It doesn't last forever. It does pass, and before you know it, you're open for business and back on the orgasm train with your lover.

Yay. Your silver lining. You're welcome. I got you, ladies and gents!

The bottom line is that you're going to feel as though your pieces will never be the same. You will worry that they'll never perform the same way. It'll seem like it hurts for days, and days, and days, likely weeks — especially if you needed stitches down there. But eventually you'll get to the point where you don't even remember pushing a tiny human out of your body, and everything will go back to normal.

This does take some time. So be patient, and remember the more you do for post-delivery care, as your doctor told you, the faster it will all get back up and running down there. When you're feeling ready for sex, give it a try. It might not work the first time, either, or you might need some assistance with the lubrication side of things. Make sure you purchase something that won't give you an infection. Meaning, don't just reach for your coconut, hemp, or avocado oil. These are all really great for your hair, for cooking with or ingesting, but orally, not vaginally. So just stick with the tried and true lubricants that you can get at your local pharmacy. (An infection is the last thing you need or want while you're caring for your brand-new human.) Also, take your time. It's probably been a long time since you lost your virginity, but try to think back to how that felt. It didn't feel great the first few times, and this will be very much the same.

And to the partner with the piece that goes in the vag? The vag that just presented you with your heir? Perhaps try a little harder on the foreplay and romance side of things, rather than leading with the classic we've-been-together-for-such-a-looooonnnnnggggg-time move of rolling over and just sticking some fingers in there. Or the old press-your-stiff-hard-dick-against-your-lover's-back/thigh/forehead-to-show-them-you're-ready move. Do some prep. Have some game, my friend. Make dinner, run them a bath, bathe the baby, tuck the baby in, light some candles, put in some effort to show your partner you're appreciative of all they're doing for you, and all they've given you. Give them a massage, shower them with sex preparation …

Take time, and put in *extra* effort for the first few times, or, you know, even for the rest of your lives. I've said too much; I'm giving away too many of my relationship secrets.

Remember when I said that when I delivered Dominique, Yannick was in New Zealand, filming a mini-series, and my mom moved in for the month before and stayed until Yannick got home and settled in, three weeks later? I had flown home before he completed production, because the thought of having a baby in a country where I had zero support system, along with an incredibly busy toddler at home, was too much to fathom. That, and we had had some pretty big, drag-down, knock-out fights about how I felt abandoned by him, down there in N.Z. all alone. (But this is not that story.) Anyway, the point is that he and I hadn't seen each other for two months. When that man arrived home, even though I had a three-week-old baby sleeping next to us, both of us were "ready to go." We couldn't have gone another minute. So, we didn't.

> Listen to your body. Have sex when you're ready.

Why am I telling you this? You might ask if I'm bragging?

No. I am not. My point is this: listen to your body. Have sex when you're ready. Don't base your sexual relationship on some average recovery time your doctor gives you. Make choices for your relationship according to your own needs, health, and knowledge.

Here is the thing about relationships, babies, and sex. A lot of couples throw sex and romance out the window when they have kids. Most couples put their babies first. Some couples, as we've discussed, even put that baby in their beds, *between* them, creating a great divide. I'm telling you not to do that — or if you do, make sure it's for as short a period as possible.

Your sexual relationship with your partner is of great importance. You glean a lot of strength from your adult relationship with your significant other. There is nobody on this planet who should rank higher than your lover, your partner, your co-creator. You are building a family *together*. So please explain to me how the notion of putting the new person in the crew into the numero uno position of importance in the family is the right choice to make. Let's all think about this for five hot minutes ... yeah, it doesn't actually make sense.

Obviously, I'm not telling you to neglect the new addition — not at all. I'm simply telling you *not* to be that couple who makes the new member the be-all and end-all of your life. You are still the adult, still in an adult, sexual relationship. That matters. The happier you and your partner are, the happier your household will be. The baby is an *addition* to your current life, not your *entire life*.

Sex is sometimes how we rediscover our partner and ourselves when life pulls us in too many directions.

Remember what we addressed at the beginning of this book, about keeping your cool? Yeah, keep doing that.

Your kid will thank you. Trust me. Try to keep this rule in place: If you treat your baby co-creator with the utmost importance and respect, you all will have a much richer, more fulfilling, more blessed life than if you don't.

The message is simple:

Have sex.

Have lots of sex.

Do not let your sex life take a back seat to your parenting life.

Even when you hate your partner, have sex. Actually, sometimes this is the *best sex.*

Sex is healing.

Sex is bonding.

Sex is the glue that will keep you together when your kids leave.

Sex is sometimes how we rediscover our partner and ourselves when life pulls us in too many directions.

It is centring.

It is healthy.

It is good for you.

Sex. Sex. Sex.

Have it. Your kids will thank you.

THINGS TO NIBBLE ON

Your partner's ear, or toe, or finger, while you're having lots of sex.

And remember to put your relationship first.

Chapter Six

House Rules and the Importance of Discipline

YOU'RE NOW GOING TO confidently give your body the time it needs to recover, so that you can get back to having lots of great sex ASAP, and you're committed to making your relationship, not your kids, the centre of your universe, so we should probably get back to talking about parenting, since that's why we're here. It's time to talk about discipline. And you can set yourself up for positive discipline right from day one.

Please, do yourself, your relationship, and your child a favour, and don't get caught up in all the BS out there: the BS that tells you this little being who has joined you on this life's journey isn't strong, amazing, resilient, and wonderful right from the get-go. It's the BS that might lead you to believe they're still too weak a being to sleep in their own beds. That they should never cry, they should never feel discomfort, they should always be looking to you and leaning on you to "show them the way." That they should never experience any sort of pain at all. That's a beautiful, utopian ideal. None of us live there.

And until we do, we need to do what's best for us. Which means we must all get our sleep so we can go out into the world and function. You're not a bad parent if you let your little one cry themselves to sleep when you first move them into their own bedroom. It makes you a parent who understands that a child who doesn't get their way by crying will eventually learn other methods of problem-solving.

> A child who doesn't get their way by crying will eventually learn other methods of problem-solving.

Let's be honest here, folks. The quickest way to get a response from anybody is to throw a loud, obnoxious fit. This usually causes the other party to act quickly, doing whatever it takes to make that fit *just stop*. It's not any different with parenting and babies. They scream. You run. It's a learned, conditioned behaviour. Think Pavlov's theory.

Are you with me?

Of course you are; you know exactly what I'm talking about. Even your dog has you figured out. I know both of my four-legged kids do. Here's a perfect example. Our dogs ring a bell on the door to alert us to their need to go outside to do their business. The bell-ringing was a brilliant trick our breeder taught them. It's awesome. There is, however, one tiny little flaw with that system: it alerts us to when the dogs want to go outside, but how do they then let us know when they want to come back *inside*?

We worked out a very simple solution to this dilemma. We trained our dogs to "speak" to come inside. This is how it works: when they're ready to come in, they return to the door and bark (translation: "hey, assholes, I'm done out here — let me back in"). How did we train them to do this, you ask? It was easy. We stood at the door, which is made of glass, and did the "speak" symbol, which they were familiar with thanks to the puppy classes we took.

(Important note here: See how we got help with rearing our dogs? Why wouldn't you do this when it comes to raising a human? Lots of people take their dogs to obedience classes — if you ain't too proud to get help with your dog, why would you be too proud to ask for it with your baby? Get help. Seek guidance. It's out there for you.)

Anyhow, back to what I was saying. Once the dogs "spoke" to come in, they were rewarded with a treat. Let me tell you that they learned super fast how to get back inside the house when they wanted to.

Why am I telling you this story? How does it pertain to your perfect, amazing child? I'll get there; bear with me.

Sometimes our dogs would go outside just to literally turn around and speak, so they could get the promised treat.

Ring the bell to go out.

Speak to come in.

Get a treat.

This went on for *hours* some days. Finally, we got our shit together. We stopped allowing our dogs to control us, and began only *randomly* rewarding the "speak" with treats. This cut the senseless in-and-out behaviour by more than half.

And now I've reached my point: it's not that different with a baby. You need to learn the signs from your kid, determine when they're taking you for a ride, and then outsmart them. Period. End of story.

Kids get insecure if they think they're smarter than their parents. You're supposed to be their superheroes, who protect them from all the evil in the world, the bogeyman in the closet, the thunder during the storm. How can they take you seriously if you cower at their fit-throwing?

You need to be their rock. You need to be the boss. This is what creates well-rounded, strong, confident individuals: your being stronger than them. Not in a physically abusive way, of course, but in an emotionally, I-know-what-I'm-doing, confident, assured, adult-in-the-room way. In the "I know what's best for you, so you are going to listen to me, and you are going to trust that I love you, and that everything I do is for your own good" way. This is you showing your kids "I got you."

> You need to be the boss. This is what creates well-rounded, strong, confident individuals.

Wake up, people. Your kids shouldn't be the boss of you. Period. End of story. Now, do not get this twisted around, as if I'm telling you to be neglectful or abusive. That is not the case and you know it, so don't even try to go down that road with me. We both know they're tiny little beings who need your protection, love, and safety. What I'm saying is that those things should not come about by you losing yourself, your relationship, and your cool.

DISCIPLINE IS NOT A DIRTY WORD

The amount of discipline to exercise in your parenting should be a direct reflection of how much you want to be able to stand your child. If you don't really want to like your kid all that much, then let them have at it: let them be free as a bird, free as an annoying, begging seagull. If you want a rock star, a lion, a person you send out into the world over whom you won't lose sleep wondering *if* they're coping, or *how* they're coping; if you want them to be somebody you admire, somebody who can weather any storm, to brave any challenge that life throws at them … then teach them the truth about life.

Teach them that you don't always win, that life isn't always easy, but that if they're brave, if they're patient, if they're willing to lose sometimes when they try, then in the end they will always win. If you want a strong, independent, healthy adult out there in the world, then you must discipline them. A lot of life isn't about failure itself, but about what you do after each failure. Let them learn this!

How do you make a lion in today's world? What I'm about to share may raise eyebrows, but I'm putting it in here anyway, because it's essential to creating a strong, independent human being. Also, it's something that's sorely lacking in modern parenting, and I believe with every fibre of my being that we need to get back to it if we want to send decent adult beings out into the world. It's the need for discipline.

Let's start at the beginning. Everybody has a different "pain threshold" for kids freaking out. I swear, the threshold of today's parents is way higher than mine or Yannick's ever was. Whining children, always moaning and complaining, seem to be fucking rampant these days. I hear them behind my house, in their yards, when they're outside "playing." Everywhere I go, out and about in the world, at the grocery store, at restaurants, I see kids who are not exactly crying but sort of moan-crying. And the parents are right there with them, just chilling, talking among themselves, listening to music, distracted on their phones, or just ignoring them. Meanwhile, I want to get involved, introduce myself, and intervene: "Will you please ask that child to communicate a *need*? Why are you letting them just walk around moaning?" But I don't, because that would be *extra* on my part.

Another new trend that is quickly becoming a personal favourite: screech playing. That running-around-shrieking-loudly-all-over-the-place thing. What is that? They aren't laughing, they aren't talking, they're just screeching. Why is letting your child dominate every single social situation a thing? A while back I was out for lunch with two of my daughters in L.A., and we watched a woman with her daughter on her lap, chatting with her girlfriend, while her kid mumbled over everything the woman was saying. It was weird. There were two things I didn't understand about this situation: 1) I didn't understand how the mother was comfortable with her baby — who was old enough to be decked out in a Burberry outfit top to bottom and able to sit in a highchair — trying to override their conversation. And 2) how was her friend finding any of it a "good time"? It was bizarre to me, and even my daughters noticed it and were wondering WTF. Yet both women seemed completely unfazed by the child loudly mumbling over their conversation. If it had been me, and that was one of my girls, I would have kindly asked them to make a choice: sit quietly colouring while sitting on my lap, or take their mumble-talk over to their high chair. I definitely wouldn't have allowed any of our girls to passive-aggressively "own me" while I was trying to also spend some time with a friend.

This might not even bother you, and that's awesome. But I want to put a thought in your head: children who want to be the centre of that sort of situation are trying to exercise their ability to *always* be the centre of your world, and they need to learn that when they go out into the world, that won't fly. When they go to daycare, or school, they won't be the centre of their teacher's world, so at a young age they might as well learn how to share attention. As a parent, you always need to step back from the scenario and ask yourself, "Is this okay? If I was at a dinner party, or in a staff meeting, and one adult in the room kept talking over everybody — or, worse, talking over the person leading the meeting — what would be my take-away impression of that person?"

I have a pretty good guess.

I'm sure you would find them incredibly rude, self-centred, and obnoxious.

This is your aha moment. If you allow your child to begin this sort of "I'm the most important person at the table" routine, *you* are sending a person just like that obnoxious co-worker out into the world. Now what do you think about nipping that behaviour in the bud?

Differently from how you originally felt about it when I brought up the L.A. lunch scene, when you thought I was maybe being a "little heavy-handed" about the entire matter, I'm sure.

Here's the thing, my friends. Don't look at raising your kid like "I'm raising a baby, and then I'm raising a toddler." Always, with everything you do as a parent, you must think, "I am raising an *adult*." Because, God willing, and assuming your kid is blessed with good health, that's what you'll end up with. If you don't want a shitty adult in your life, then don't raise one.

As you know, Yannick and I were super-young parents. And because we were so young, we parented with a throwback method. Not many do it this way anymore, but we were spankers. We didn't hit our girls; we didn't yell or scream or grab them (well, once they were teenagers, we might've been known to lose our cool now and then). When they were little, before hormones came and stole our easygoing girls away, we had organized discipline. It was organized because we had three simple house rules:

1) Don't lie
2) Don't disrespect
3) Don't disobey

Some of you might be having thoughts like, "Wow, I never would have bought this book if I knew she was pro spanking — that's child abuse." Or maybe, "Where is their individual freedom if they aren't allowed to express themselves by disagreeing with you?"

Look, these are all valid questions and concerns. You don't need to spank your kid if you don't want to. But believe me when I tell you that parenting them with *zero* consequences for stepping outside the rules isn't the way to go, either. Why not, you ask? I'll tell you. It isn't the way to parent because the world doesn't work that way. When they don't hand in a school project in the allotted time, the teacher isn't going to give them extra time with zero consequences. They will most likely lose a percentage of their grade for every day they don't hand in the project. In the real adult world, an employer won't keep them around very long if they throw a fit every single time they're asked to perform their duties. I know you can attest to this.

Do you see what I'm getting at here?

Many of today's parenting methods have a short-game mentality. Helicopter parenting — hovering over them; not allowing them to learn anything about life through their own organic experience of it — is stealing from them. You're literally taking away all the exploration of self-discovery or of using their own brain for problem-solving by doing it for them. This includes inserting yourself into your child's school life. It is not your job to do their homework, or their projects. This is not your chance to redo elementary school and really shine. This is for your child. Let them struggle. Let them problem-solve. Let them go back to their teacher for extra help. Let them learn to live without you holding their hand and fighting their battles.

> Coddling them breeds insecurity; it tells them that you know they cannot do it on their own.

You're not always going to be around, so make sure you give them what they need to succeed. A big part of that is trusting in their own ability to get to the other side of a problem, by finding the solution themselves. Think back to your childhood: how much would you have liked it if your parents buffered everything that you actually had the opportunity to learn on your own? Figuring shit out by yourself is empowering! It makes a kid feel like a super-human. Coddling them breeds insecurity; it tells them that you know they cannot do it on their own and that's why you *must* do it for them. Not cool.

Then we have the lovely lawnmower parent, who is constantly buffering life for their child so that everything for the kid is smooth sailing; there's no hardship to endure. These parents are mowing difficulties out of their children's lives, clearing the way of any and all hardships.

Neither of these methods is going to create strong, resilient adults. In the moment, the child may feel better with your safety net there to catch them, or never knowing struggle. But I'm writing this book to give you a *long-game* mentality. You will make a better human. All of you will have fuller, richer lives. Parenting, my friends, is about …

Balance.

If you don't want to spank, then don't, but be sure you teach them that for every action, there is a reaction or consequence. If they disrespect you by mouthing off at you, they should receive a punishment. Why? I'll tell you again: when they go out into the world, and their teacher or their boss challenges them on where their homework is or why they didn't get their part of a contract completed on time, they need to be able to accept responsibility. If you never teach them that an authority figure's words and expectations are to be honoured, they won't do it outside your house. Trust me on this. Your house rules set them up for how they will behave in the world. They will never take responsibility for dropping the ball in their lives if you don't teach them how to accept responsibility for it in their own home. They will become "buck-passers." If you own a company, or if you've ever worked as part of a team, I'm sure you've encountered someone who is not responsible for their part — the person who loves to "pass the buck" of blame onto somebody else, who has zero humility, and won't accept responsibility when they drop the ball.

Now, can we all take a moment to consider how we feel about people like this? Are these the people you want to have over for dinner? The sort you want to invite to a pro-sports game with you?

No.

No, you do not want to chill with these people. You want to wring their necks.

Now, let me ask you this. Is this the kind of person you want to put out into the world? This beautiful, wonderful, amazing soul you've brought into this world, the little human you would lay your life down for. Do you want them to become one of these people?

No, you do not.

And you know why I know you do not? Because right at the beginning of this book, you promised that you wouldn't lose your cool PBA. And if you're a lazy, indulgent parent, you'll be the opposite of cool: you'll be uncool. I know it, and you know it. So, do your job.

Don't take any shortcuts. Discipline them. Be consistent, and be fair. Be organized in your discipline. In other words, have house rules. In our house, everybody knew what "crossing the line" was, and what the punishment would be if they decided to break the rules. If you discipline like this, you will have a home with much less drama in it. I know; I created a home like this. You won't get to that snapping, breaking, seeing-red parenting point, where you lash out at them verbally or, God forbid, physically, over and over again. If you have a system in place, you will always be able to calmly look at your child and ask them if they feel as though their current attitude, choice, or behaviour is breaking any of your rules. Once they reply, you then just calmly say, "Okay. You've broken a house rule. You know what happens next ..."

Then you hand out whatever your partner and you have determined to be enough punishment to fit the crime.

There's no rage.

No violence.

No anger.

No judgment.

Just regular, real, outside-the-walls-of-your-family-home life, where every action causes a reaction, so they better get ready for it.

When you don't teach your child about consequences, you're truly setting them up for failure. The big, beautiful world we all love and live in doesn't operate within the same bubble we have within our own home. If you don't teach your kids how to be told "no," or that they aren't the coolest, brightest, bestest kid out there, you really are setting them up for disappointment.

THE IMPORTANCE OF INSTILLING VALUES

Many people think structure and rules squash the child's spirit. They might say that you're instilling your beliefs into an independent soul, and that that's not your place as a parent. That your job as a parent is to bring your children into this world, give them food, shelter, and love, and then be there to catch them when they fall.

That's bullshit.

I always try to get parents to think about it differently. To parents with that philosophy, I ask, "Do you tell your child not to murder? Or cause harm to their fellow human?" Most often, they say that of course they teach their child not to harm other people. To which I ask, "So what's the difference?" I mean really, what is the difference between instilling that belief in them and instilling other core beliefs? Such as, *don't lie, don't be disrespectful, be kind*, or whatever else you deem an important quality for your little human to have.

The answer is that there's zero difference. If you insist to your child that you don't want them wearing their shoes in the house, but their best friend has parents who couldn't care less about shoes, then you've "put" something on your kid that other people don't necessarily give a damn about. So, don't kid yourself, you uber free-thinking, liberal parents. You are putting shit on your kids all the time. We all are. We all like to think we're teaching open-mindedness and complete tolerance, but it's very hard to be judgment free. The important thing is to make sure your kid understands that being taught decent core values is not the same as being judged or stifled. And that they do learn to be kind, tolerant, and open minded. It's a very tricky balance!

But you know all that, right?

ISN'T DISCIPLINE JUST TELLING THEM THEY'RE NOT GOOD ENOUGH?

This is so not true. Discipline creates exactly what you want it to: strength and changed behaviour. For example, consider the Olympics, and the gymnasts sticking their clean landings after a perfect floor or balance-beam routine. Or my friend Tessa Virtue, the most decorated figure skater on the planet. Or the hockey team that wins the Stanley Cup. Or the football team that brings home the coveted Super Bowl trophy. How is a champion made? By being told that their last effort wasn't "good enough." By being told to go back and try that floor routine "one more time" until it's gold-medal worthy. You build a champion, a winner — somebody who gets the most out of their lives — by calling them higher. By asking them to not settle for their minimal effort. By telling them that you expect the truth out of them when you ask them a question. By letting them know that squealing or crying will not get them what they want. That if they want you to do something for them, or if they want something from you, they need to communicate clearly, respectfully, and intelligently to get a positive outcome.

We admire the win at any cost in our athletes, but for some reason we want to let our own kids "off the hook" of excellence by not being hard enough on them. This goes back to what I said earlier: "If you want your kid to grow into an adult whom you and other people will love to spend time with, discipline them. If you never want to see them again once you send them out into the world, then be a lazy parent." The choice is yours.

> Discipline creates exactly what you want it to: strength and changed behaviour.

Your kid has one life: why not raise a champion? I'm not telling you that you can't believe the sun shines out of your kid's ass as they are: pro-athlete, Olympian, or couch potato. I have three, and although they drive me crazy from time to time, I still think they deserve the best this life has to offer them. I believe wholeheartedly that they're the smartest, most wonderful, amazing people I know. But I still call them on their bullshit — even now, and they're thirty-one, twenty-nine, and twenty-three. I don't let them off the hook at all when they're being assholes, and you know what? They don't let me off the hook when *I'm* being an asshole, either. They can do that, because they trust me and know that I'm their greatest fan, and I trust them and believe they're pretty fond of me, too.

Your kid isn't likely to be top student in their class, or captain of their sports team. Not everybody can have these roles in society. Most of us fall somewhere in the middle. We do our best, as best we can. My girls weren't the captains of teams, or members of Mensa. Did this make me love them any less?

No, it did not. And it won't make you love your kid any less, either.

HELP THEM LEARN FROM THEIR MISTAKES

When disciplining our girls, we always had a dialogue about it. It went like this: the girls would break a house rule. We would catch them. We would then ask them, "Do you understand what you just did?"

Nine times out of ten, they would look at us and reply, "Yes, I do."

"Okay. Can you explain it to me?" we would ask.

Then, based on which rule they broke, they would answer us. We would explain to them that breaking that rule had consequences. They would get three spanks on their bum (fully clothed), and then they would have a cry. We would hug them and be with them until they stopped crying. Afterward, we would ask them how they felt about what they had done, and how they felt about the consequence. We also asked them to share with us how they could have made different choices, and what they would do differently if this situation presented itself to them again down the road.

All the way along, we had conversations to help them understand that they had the power to problem-solve. That it was up to them, and was forever in their power, to choose how they reacted to an upsetting situation. We gave them the tools to express themselves clearly and taught them that they didn't need to go through life at the mercy of their emotional reactions to a situation. We enabled them to step back, survey the situation, and handle it in a controlled way, rather than with an out-of-control reaction. We taught them to not just live their lives off their emotions. We taught our daughters how not to live a reactive life, victims of how people did or didn't talk to them. It taught them how to stop, take stock of what they were feeling and thinking in the situation, and decide whether it warranted an emotional outburst. They developed the art of self-control during a conflict, which is an extremely important life skill to have, out in the real world with bosses, professors, friends, and partners.

Trust me, you don't want a kid who lives as if every feeling they have is *fact*. It is not. Feelings come; feelings go. Do your kids the favour of teaching them how to have feelings, process them, and deal with them in a healthy way. We always had a dialogue to help them understand when they began to feel upset, and at what point along the way they could have handled it in a more constructive way. Not just to resolve things with friends and family, but for their own internal peace. We always showed them that they had other options for handling themselves, so they'd be prepared if the same scenario cropped up again.

We didn't just spank them; we taught them. We didn't just give them a punishment; we gave them knowledge. We didn't just tell them how to be; we asked them how they wanted to be. We gave them tools. Tools to cope in a stressful situation without losing their cool. Tools to express themselves with words instead of emotion. We equipped them with knowledge so they would understand that every action has a reaction, and not all of them are good. We taught them to be mindful of how they behaved inside the house, and outside of it.

Live this yourself and teach it to your kids. We are making full, strong, confident individuals who will one day go out in the world and fend for themselves, independent and sure. We are raising the next generation of leaders.

Your kid will be their own person. They will excel where they excel, and fail where they fail. But ultimately, if they are supported, if they are disciplined — with love — they will survive both their successes and failures. You see, you don't want to raise a person who can deal only with being successful. You want them to be able to manage anything life throws at them. Life is messy, and unexpected, and sometimes just plain awful. They need to know how to deal with every part of it, not just the good stuff.

WHAT SHOULD OUR HOUSE RULES BE?

Sit down with your significant other to hash out the things that matter most to you. What are the character traits that you simply cannot tolerate in people you come across in the world? Only the two of you can decide what you don't want your little human to emulate.

You will most likely have differences of opinion as to what irks you most. This is why it's important to pick only a few house rules. It's a good idea to pick character traits that would generally piss off most of the world, and would therefore cause you to want to implement a disciplinary action. Don't go crazy. Don't have so many rules that your kid needs a whiteboard and a PowerPoint presentation to keep track of them. The most important part of house rules is that they are instilled.

Once you've picked them, make a HOUSE RULES sign and put it where everybody can see it, then stick to it. By sticking to the house rules and the consequences that go with them, you have little to zero chance of having "snapping" attacks against your kid when you've finally had enough of their shitty behaviour. Having a system of rules ensures that infractions are handled the same way every time, and that the situation is dealt with swiftly and compassionately. No grudges held by either party. Both are free to carry on with their day once the rule-breaking has been dealt with. And for God's sake, be consistent.

> Don't have so many rules that your kid needs a whiteboard to keep track of them.

This, my friends, is the most difficult part of parenting. You're probably thinking, "Two or three rules to keep track of can't be that tough. I mean, how hard can it actually be?" Well, let me tell you, it is damn hard once you have more than one kid in the house, or when the days are long and you're parenting solo for whatever reason, so you let the kids get away with "a little lie," or you let them tell you "no" when you ask them to do the dishes, just once, 'cos you're tired and it's actually, more often than not, easier to do it yourself.

My friends, you cannot do this. You cannot let them tell you the way it's going to be. You have your rules and *you* must follow them so that *they* will follow them. You have to be consistent. If you want groovy adults to chill with, you have to put in all the hard work now. Don't give up; don't slack. Get the job done. You can do this. I know you can, because you're awesome, and you've maintained your cool thus far. Why stop now?

THE ART OF TELLING THEM *NO*

All right, this is an important thing to be able to do — again if you want to raise a human being who doesn't have an anxiety attack when they're told *no* by somebody out in the real world. Because even if you *swore* you would *never, ever* tell your children *no* — maybe because you had autocratic parents who lorded their parentdom over you, who automatically said *no* when you asked for the simplest thing, never giving a reason because, after all, they were the parents, so they naturally knew better about absolutely everything there was to know about on the planet — you actually do have to learn to say *no.*

Now that you're all grown up, and have lived a little, gone out in the world and seen the way it actually operates outside your family's four walls, you've learned that not all grown-ups do in fact know better. Some adults are pure jackasses, and when they open their mouths, the dumbest shit falls out. Perhaps you were raised by one of these, in which case I totally get why you made the commitment to never be that person. I respect that. I did the same thing after growing up in a home with one alcoholic parent, and so, yeah, I'm not an alcoholic. But saying *no* is not the same as that. Children have to hear the word *no* because, simply put, they cannot have everything their way; nor should they get everything they want. That is not real life.

But what if you end up with a child who just doesn't accept the word *no* as an answer? What do you do then? When you have that kid who's like a woodpecker, just pecking, pecking, pecking away at you. Asking. Asking again. Asking ... asking ... asking. They wear you down. You even forget why you said *no* in the first place ... so you give in and say *yes*. And so begins your child's education: if they ask enough times, if they can simply outlast you and not give up their quest, they will eventually win. Persistence in and of itself is not a bad thing. But this child can wear a parent down to where they just want to wave the white flag and say yes to every single request to prevent another battle. Parenting can make you battle weary, especially if you've been gifted with one of these kids. Listen, I get it. We gave birth to one of those kids, and there were days we were so exhausted from the cycle of saying *no* that we came up with a family rule about it.

Yannick and I finally came up with something that was fair to all of us and also allowed the girls to feel like they were being heard when they asked for something. It went like this: they asked, we considered the request. Upon reflection, if we determined that it was going to be a *no*, we had to provide them with three reasons. We called a family meeting and told everybody the new standard. Everybody thought that was fair.

It was incredibly interesting to see how this system brought out hidden character traits in our girls. We often had heated debates in which they countered our reasons with their own arguments. This system inadvertently taught our girls three things:

1) The ability to argue your point is a skill that you will always use in life. The art of negotiation is always in fashion, especially when you can do it without crying or throwing a fit to "get your way."

2) Sometimes you think you want something, but upon hitting an obstacle, you come to realize that you actually don't want or need it at all — this lesson also helped us avoid breeding impulse shoppers.

3) It's invaluable to be able to not only hear but also understand somebody else's position on a matter.

All of these are important skills for children to develop at an early age — tools they will take with them as they move through life.

MY PARTNER AND I CAN'T AGREE — NOW WHAT?

Okay, I don't want to be rude, but I wish I had known you before this book, and before Junior joined your world. I would have instructed you to have these conversations *before* your baby arrived, because truly, they are way more important than the "where do you want to buy a house" conversation.

But since we're here now, I suggest you get an amazing family therapist and sit down with them and discuss how to bridge this parenting gap. In my humble, non-professional opinion, nothing is more important than knowing how your partner wants to parent and finding methods that you can agree on. Like a great country (you and your partner) in the presence of a great foe (your kid), you will fall if you are divided. You must be unified going into it. Children can smell your fear, or any disunity or dissension. If they do, they will divide and conquer. Figure your shit out as a couple and do it quickly. No child should ever have a foothold, or the ability to divide their parents.

> Nothing is more important than knowing how your partner wants to parent and finding methods that you can agree on.

And for the love of God, do *not* undermine one another in front of your kid. Maybe hubby is flying off the handle, or Momma Bear is grumpy and impatient, but whatever the reason, one of you *will* blow it with your kid. More than once. You/your partner will snap at them, with not a whole lot of love or patience in your tone, or make some angry punishment decision that the kid really doesn't deserve. This will happen, because you're human. And when it does, you must not challenge your partner in front of the kid(s). I'm telling you, you cannot. It's hard, because you know they're blowing it, but hold off. You criticizing your partner is one of the worst things for a kid to witness; you never want them to think that the two of you aren't a team.

Now, this is not the same thing as never admitting to them that you're wrong. That's totally different. When something like this happens, you need to follow it up by having a family meeting and explaining to your kid that parent 1 was "disrespectful" when they argued with parent 2. Apologize to both your kid and your partner at the family meeting so they see you being humble. They will see that even though you made a mistake, they're not to get it twisted: you parents are still a team. You must always be humble and take ownership when you're wrong — another great opportunity to teach them that there's no shame in being wrong. We're all human, and we all make mistakes. If they witness you admitting that you fuck up from time to time, they won't feel helpless or like a failure when they do it.

Here's a prime example. One of my greatest flaws is that I don't naturally "listen"; I'm more of a talker. The way this presented as a problem in our parenting was that I often liked to do the disciplinary talking during family meetings, which in and of itself wasn't horrible, except when my talking was undermining something Yannick was saying. I always thought he was too stern and unreasonable with Dominique, so if he was giving her a talking-to, it was not uncommon for me to express my disagreement out loud.

I had to do a lot of apologizing, not only to Dominique for sending her confused messages, but also, and primarily, to Yannick.

Which brings me to the crux of this point: it's totally uncool to undermine your partner's authority in front of your kid. Because if you undermine them, guess what that is teaching your child?

You got it.

It teaches them that they too can undermine the other parent. It shows them that their parent doesn't know what the hell they're doing, and that if the parent was wrong, then the kid's behaviour must be right — even Mommy or Daddy thinks so. You must, at all costs — even if it means biting your lip until you draw blood — wait until the kid is in bed, or at the very least in another room, to address it with your partner.

I'm sure some of you reading this right now have been instantly transplanted to an exact scenario like this in your own young life. You fucked up in some way, and one parent overreacted and then the other parent stepped in to save the day. Remember how satisfied you were to see your parent "getting in trouble" instead of you, even though you really did deserve the heat?

Yeah, you do.

Do not repeat this pattern. Be sure to always present a united front, even when it's not. This is a big, big deal, folks. If you get to the point where you feel like you're going to burst and let your partner have it, do everyone a favour and *leave the room*. I've done this way too many times to Yannick and, honestly, it's a long climb out of the hole. A long climb out of a muddy hole while wearing ballet slippers. So don't do it.

United we stand, divided we fall.

Your kid(s) must know without a doubt that your relationship is the most important one to both of you, that you cannot be divided on a whim by them throwing a fit or misbehaving. Children glean so much security from knowing that their parents are tight. That they are a team. That they, together, are unshakable. Even when a kid doesn't get their way, trust me when I tell you that this actually makes them feel more secure and confident than if they had won. Think about it. I know you know kids aren't supposed to be the boss of adults. I mean, how would that even work?

Your kid(s) must know that your relationship is the most important one to both of you.

It wouldn't. It doesn't. Kids instinctively know that you're supposed to be in charge, so don't let them down. Don't make your kids insecure by leaving them out there blowing in the wind, trying to figure out "right from wrong" or the difference between "acceptable" and "unacceptable" behaviour all on their own. Love them enough to show them the way.

Do your job. Be in charge.

And remember to have sex.

THINGS TO NIBBLE ON

Understand the importance of establishing structure in your child's life, to set them up to go out into the world and be successful, happy, confident, strong individuals who add to the world rather than burden it.

Do not be afraid to discipline them. You are not here to be their friends. If you raise and parent them well, that will come later, and naturally. But for right now, you have work to do.

Teach them to express themselves in a positive, productive way, rather than getting their own way simply because they wore you down until you just couldn't argue about it any longer.

Don't overwhelm them with too many house rules. Pick the two or three that are most important to you and your partner.

Whatever you do, don't argue about how either one of you is disciplining your kid when the kid is in the middle of getting in trouble.

If you truly can't agree on the rules or how to discipline, then seek help from a family therapist — they can work wonders.

If you disagree and keep your disagreeing mouth shut, you know what happens? You're both happier, which makes it so much easier to *have sex.*

Chapter Seven

Toddler to Double Digits

YOUR LITTLE BLOB OF A HUMAN now walks around, talks to you, and has their own personality. You've established a deep bond and are a real family now. How quickly time flies. By this point you've established yourself as a tough but fair parent. You have a short list of easy house rules that you and your partner agree on, and the kid knows what the consequences will be if and when they break those rules. And you're committed to never throwing each other under the bus in the presence of the kids.

> From when your kid is a toddler until they hit double digits, these are the groundwork years.

From when your kid is a toddler until they hit double digits, I like to call these the groundwork years. These are the years when you really need to be on your parenting A-game. These are the years in which they will challenge you, and push you on whether your rules are really here to stay, or when you taught them, were you just a windbag who liked the sound of your own voice.

You started — or hopefully you started — when they were very small. Hopefully, the first time your kid attempted to own you via manipulation, by throwing baby temper tantrums, you didn't stand for it. If you didn't stand for it, I'm incredibly proud of you. You regularly completed the whole healthy baby check, sort of like your safe-car check before you head out on a long road trip. You checked their bums, and they were dry. You tried to feed them, and they weren't hungry. You checked their teeth and gave them some soothing teething gel, "just in case." Yet something you couldn't see was still upsetting them, and they were still screaming. I know you looked them in their little eyes, told them that they were fine, told them to calm down, held them close to reassure them they were safe. You did all the positive, healthy parenting things you needed to do. Hopefully, you managed to get them to stop freaking out; but if you didn't, you did one final thing. You took your clearly exhausted baby and laid said baby in bed for a nap. Because if all that other stuff was good, then you knew your baby was just tired. Even if they lay there crying for five, ten, fifteen minutes, trying to prove to you that you don't know shit … you *did* know shit. Every time, you said *I am the parent; I got this, and I'm awesome*. You didn't let this small human in your life cause you to doubt yourself. You trusted yourself.

By addressing all the things that could possibly have been wrong, and then teaching them that they now needed to calm down, you were laying the groundwork for them to build coping skills. If you did this with them when they were very small, then you can expect it to translate into every aspect of their lives.

I hate to do this to you, again, but honestly, it's such a great reference for human parents to grasp, as so many of us have had a dog at least once in our lifetimes. So, here we go: parenting your child, who initially has zero vocabulary, is extremely similar to raising a pup. Both rely on you to teach them the art of communicating with you through repetition. A child will never learn that throwing a fit is not the best way to get your attention if you pick up that child every single time it screams its fool head off. It's the same with a pup. When you bring a puppy home and it howls that first night away in its crate, what do you do? Do you go down and rescue it, bring it into your bedroom because it's lonely and scared? I hope to hell you do not. I hope you go downstairs, reassure the pup that you're still here, that it's safe, and tell it to quiet down and go to sleep now.

That's what we do every time we bring a new dog into our lives, and let me tell you this: within a couple of nights, all of us are sleeping through the night. You assert yourself by communicating to the pup the expectation of behaviour, then you back that up by hugging it, kissing it, and telling the puppy that "it's fine, you're safe, you are *okay.*" Then you kiss it one more time, tuck it back into its new bed, turn off the lights, and head back upstairs.

And just like with your human baby, it doesn't happen just once. Your pup tests you. It howls again and again in its attempt to get you to come back downstairs and take it out of the crate. But you do not do this. Instead, you head back downstairs and go over the entire scenario again, and again, and again, until you have a pup who knows that you're the boss. And that crate time is sleep time, and in the morning the sun will shine, and you will all be together again. This is the positive reinforcement of love, trust, and obedience.

You have to do the same thing with your child. Over and over again, until they get it. And get it they will, but you must not give up, you must not doubt, and you cannot quit, even if you were gifted with an extremely strong-willed child, as we were.

Keep at it with love, and you will all be the better for it. You're in this phase of what I like to call repetitive parenting, where it seems like your kid is just never going to listen to you. Where you sound like a broken record; where even you hate the sound of your own voice. They're asking you the same question sometimes twelve times a day, and you try to mix up your responses to them, trying out your best high-school drama improv. Anything at all to help you not lose your cool. But you do start to believe, you are absolutely convinced, that your baby or child will *never listen*, and you're bouncing between giving up and maybe

You're in this phase of what I like to call repetitive parenting, where it seems like your kid is just never going to listen to you.

wanting to die, confident that there's no way in hell you're going to get to the other side of this stage. Trust me, you will. We all do.

But the one surefire way to ensure that you don't get to the other side of fit-throwing is to quit. To stop parenting them through it. If you leave them to their own devices, you will have reinforced their negative behaviour, and that'll be on you. So, put in the work now. It will feel exhausting while you're in it, but when you're that parent on an airplane *not* handing out apology bags to all the other travellers because you know you've never allowed your child to get away with screaming their heads off, think of how cool you'll feel then? Super cool. Trust me, I know. I was always that cool parent whose children were not throwing their tiny weight around a crowded space filled with other human beings.

So, weird as it may sound, parent your kid the same way you parent your dog. Just as you don't want your dog to control the dynamics of your entire family, you don't want your toddler running roughshod over you. If you can expect this of your dog, why can't you expect it of your own flesh and blood? The answer is you can — you just need to decide to do it and then see it through. Every time. There's no reason that you need to be out and about in the world with your two-year-old, apologizing everywhere you go because your kid is a holy fucking terror, kicking, screaming, yelling, punching at you and, God forbid, other people. That's gross. You know it's gross. You used to think it was gross before you had your own precious child, so what's changed? The short answer is *nothing*; you still think it's gross behaviour for a child to display. So, parent it out of them.

And while we're on this subject, do you mind if I take two minutes to ask what is up with parents allowing this behaviour to go on? I see this in public way too much these days, and let me tell you, as a parent who has gone before you, not only is it repulsive, but you are also doing a huge disservice to your child. Nobody is going to want to play with them, and worse, when they grow up, nobody will hire them if they can't keep their emotions in check. It is your fault if your kid is a brat, not your kid's fault. Your kid will give you opportunity after opportunity to parent them. Every day of their little lives, they will test you, to check to see if you mean business. So, you better mean what you say and say what you mean, because if you don't, your kid is going to be the first person to call your bluff. And suffer the consequences of your lazy parenting.

There is no reason on this earth why you or anyone else should say, "Oh, she's just in her terrible twos …" No. That's a cop-out for lazy parenting. I've had three daughters, all three incredibly strong-willed young women. Even as babies they all had their own minds, their own ideas, and it was our job to raise them in a way that allowed them the freedom to express themselves without being abusive to anybody around them.

Which takes us perfectly to the next point of this chapter.

TEACH THEM, BY SHOWING THEM, HOW TO FIGHT FAIR

Teach your child to fight fair, because everybody is going to fight, but it doesn't have to get ugly, ever. In our home we never, ever allowed verbal abuse. I've seen so many kids who were not given the gift of being taught how to fight fair. Going back to our three house rules, this fell under the *no disrespect* rule. Our girls were allowed to get angry, they were allowed to disagree, they were allowed to express their opinions and feelings, but they had to do it kindly. Not perfectly, not necessarily calmly, just respectfully. They were allowed to raise their voices, to cry, to challenge one another and us, but man oh man, if they hit below the belt or called names, no sirree, *no*. That was grounds for discipline. It is one of the most important parts of the job, to teach your children how to fight fair.

They learn it by seeing it, too, so go all the way back to the section in this book that talks about having humility in your relationship with their other parent. The way you fight and work through disagreements is how they will, too, so make sure you show them the right way, with kindness and with love. Fight with love even when you're angry — *especially* when you're angry. Speak your truth with love; you'll get much farther that way. (You'll also end up with a happier relationship, because it won't suffer any damage if you fight fair.) Giving your kid this life skill early on is one of the greatest gifts you can bestow on them. Think about how well it will go for them as high school or college students when they're dealing with a teacher who has a difficult personality. Some teachers simply do, just like anyone else. Think about how your child will handle it if they have indeed been treated unfairly, and they need to

> I've seen so many kids who were not given the gift of being taught how to fight fair.

go and get that grade they know they deserved. If they have the skill of fighting for what they want in a calm, articulate way, they will have a much better chance with that teacher. They'll know how to persuasively advocate for themselves.

Which brings me to a sidebar … don't ever, *ever*, contact a teacher to fight about your kid's report card or project. That is so uncool. The very definition of uncool. And this book is all about how to keep the cool you had *before* you became a parent, so don't do it. Ever. Let them fight their own battles. If you've done your job, they will have acquired the skills they need at home. Trust me, I watch our girls go out and get what they want from difficult personalities all the time, using the fight-fair skills we gave them. These skills are invaluable. Start young. Make them talk shit through rather than just throw their fists and raise their voices. Ain't nobody getting that grade they're after with those tactics!

TEACH THEM TO LOVE THE PLANET WITHOUT THEM LOSING SLEEP

Which brings us naturally to a very important thing that is happening in school these days: the bombardment, pressure, and intensity with which our kids are being told that it is their job to "save our planet." Okay. Listen, I love Mother Earth. I pray daily about my deep gratitude to her for the way she sustains us, amazes us, blesses us with her beauty and her abundance of natural resources. She has taken amazing care of us, so yes, we need to thank her with our actions and do better to preserve every part of her. You'll never get an argument out of me about that.

But. And this is a big but: I think we can educate our children without giving them nightmares about the end of the world. We need to back off on *how much* of this we dump on them, and *when*.

I'm not talking about the great debate about whether it's true ("science is wrong," "there's no data on coal being a major cause of greenhouse gases," blah, blah, blah, on and on and on it goes). Are we abusing her? Yes, we are. Is there a very real danger of it all coming to an end? I also say yes. But even though we know this is true, we shouldn't drive our elementary school kids to drink by making it their burden to carry. Our girls were the first generation to reduce, recycle, reuse. It was awesome. We all learned together how we could be more respectful of our one and only planet. We were the first generation, and since then I have seen the intensity of the curriculum change so much that it borders on hysteria.

We all need to calm down.

There is a way to instill respect for Mother Earth in our children without overwhelming them right onto Xanax. I believe that we can educate them about climate change urgency in the same way we educate boys and girls about sex (which is coming up right after this): naturally. Organically. And gently. Use opportunities that come up in your day-to-day life to teach them how to make a difference to our planet. As you're walking down the street, you can pick up trash together; or when you're brushing your teeth, you can talk about shutting off the water. Show them that you turn off lights when you leave a room; make it a house rule not to use single-use plastic bottles or bags. Lead by example, the same way you lead in every other aspect of life. 'Cos you're doing that already, right? Right?

Yeah, I know you are. Yay, you.

If you have a child who gets overwhelmed and scares easily, like our youngest, then talk to their teachers about educating your child without sending them down nightmare alley. We all know your one kid can't possibly save the whales and the puffins, get water to Africa, and stop human trafficking all on their own. But they can certainly do their part, and that's the best they can do. Every little bit does help and does count, and that's the message you want them to learn.

TALKING ABOUT THE BIRDS AND THE BEES

What about sex education? Man oh man, this is a loaded gun. Everybody has sex, but nobody wants to acknowledge to their own kids that they do.

Weird.

I mean, I get it, you don't want to leave the bedroom door open while you're getting it on, and you don't want to have sex in front of your kids. Actually, I do have friends who will have sex in a hotel room when their kids are asleep in the other bed. That was never my style. I would always worry that they might wake up and wonder what the actual fuck was going on with Mommy and Daddy. That wasn't a visual I ever wanted my kids to have. Bad enough they've heard us through plenty of walls — they imparted that fact to us over a recent family dinner ... *awkward* — but being in the same room? Nah. Sorry, I don't go for that.

Now, having a shower while they're sleeping and getting it on in there, yes. I've done that. What you're comfortable with is up to you, but I do suggest a level of discretion when staying in the same room, which is another reason why I'm not a fan of the whole family bed business. You do see what I'm saying here? And now we know that it increases the risk of SIDS … let's just keep kids in their own beds, shall we?

Now, what the hell to do about sex talks with your kid? Yannick and I had a very casual approach to sex. We never sat the girls down and had "the talk," but that's because the topic of sex was an ongoing dialogue in our house. The girls knew they had vaginas, and that Daddy, and all boys, had penises. They knew that you needed a man and a woman to make a baby. They had baths with their dad when they were little, probably until like age four, and with me, too. We walked around naked after showers, and they would sit on our beds chatting with us while we got dressed. There was no shame attached to the naked body, and sex was just something that was. It was neither taboo, nor overly celebrated. It just was.

We had the attitude that we wanted to be the people to talk to them about sex, so we were. It wasn't until they were older, around middle school, that we had to begin addressing questions about what oral sex and anal sex were, or about friends who were lesbian or gay. We talked frankly about these issues. We let them ask, and we would answer, honestly. In my opinion, in dealing with the topic of sex, honesty and openness are key. After all, I'm confident you'd prefer their sex education to come from a safe place of love, with people they can trust, rather than from the internet. And from what I'm hearing from friends who are just beginning this journey into the double digits, the questions are coming in younger and younger, so you and your partner better have a plan for how you'll deal with the topic sooner rather than later.

I will touch on the topic of gender identity ever so briefly, as I have no hands-on experience with this, nor do we have any kids thus far in the family who have needed guidance through the challenging and scary journey of coming out as who they truly are. But what I know is how very important it is to teach our kids that not all of us are made the same, and that it's okay.

In dealing with the topic of sex, honesty and openness are key.

It is so crucial to teach our children about inclusivity from a very young age and to instill in them a judgment-free attitude about things that people cannot control. We need to teach them to let people be who they are, as long as they aren't harming anybody, in the same way they would want people to let them be *their* authentic selves. The health of our society as a whole depends on each one of us teaching our children how to live without judging others.

What I do advise in this situation is the same thing I advise whenever you feel out of your depth as a parent: the best thing you can ever do for your child at any time during their development, whenever they reveal something that you're not equipped to deal with, is to get them a professional to talk to as quickly as possible. If finances are an issue, check with the guidance counsellor at their school, or go online and get informed about free helplines or communities that can help you support and navigate the process. As parents, our priority should always be ensuring that our children feel safe. No matter what they're feeling, what they're confused or hurting about, we must be their shelter in the storm. If you cannot be, for whatever reason, then I strongly suggest you find them somebody who can.

What's next on this chapter's agenda?

Oh yeah.

SWEET, ELUSIVE SLEEP

Sleep eludes many children. There are some basic tricks parents try, like not feeding them too close to bedtime to avoid digestion issues or the need to wake to pee in the night. But sometimes, nothing works. You can engage the child in relaxing, quiet, meditative activities close to bedtime. You can give them a warm soak in the tub, a quiet storytime, a light massage, and gentle, soothing music, but still your kid will not sleep. I know I've mentioned this a trillion times, but our eldest, Brianna, didn't sleep well. We thought all her digestion issues and terrible sleeping patterns were just "normal" little-kid behaviours. They weren't, but we didn't know enough to understand that or seek more specialized medical advice. Her sleep problems have followed her into adulthood, and we still haven't found a way to help her sleep better. She's thirty-one now and still needs to use multiple techniques to help her sleep.

> Do all you can to calm your child throughout the evening hours.

But even if there are real, underlying medical reasons, I believe you should still do all you can to calm your child throughout the evening hours, particularly if they are troubled sleepers. Limit or avoid sugar entirely in their diets. Create a Zen- and qi-friendly bedroom for them. Feng shui offers suggestions for paint colours that help soothe and calm, and even recommendations about which wall to set the child's headboard against and which direction their feet should be pointing while they sleep. Declutter their bedroom so they're not overwhelmed by the energy of stuff around them while they sleep. Yannick and I engage in all of these practices for ourselves and for the most part enjoy deep, fulfilling sleep each and every night. Our daughter, on the other hand, sleeps in a terribly cluttered room, filled to the brim with stuff. I believe that's her biggest problem, but hey, why would she listen to me? I'm just her mom.

Remember that awesome, rock-star doctor or health practitioner you picked for yourself while pregnant? Lean on them; ask them lots of questions. You can also seek out holistic remedies to aid your child's sleep. You don't have to fill your child with prescription pills; there are plenty of herbal and vitamin options at your disposal. Even something as gentle as mild lavender water sprayed on your child's pillow can help calm and soothe.

And for the love of God, do not follow the sitting-in-the-hall-right-outside-their-door-until-they-fall-asleep "sleep training" bullshit trend. My friends, this is the epitome of child-parent manipulation. Who's in charge in that scenario? It definitely isn't the parent. And if you think your kid was insecure before you sat out in that hallway, how secure do you think they're going to feel knowing that they're in control of *you*? I'm pretty sure you know the answer.

Are you going to go to university with them and sit outside their dorm room until they fall asleep when they're going through stressful times? No. No, you are not. So don't enable this sleep pattern now. Teach them how to self-soothe and fall asleep on their own, no matter the situation they find themselves in.

And another thing: put down the cellphones, the iPads, the computers, and the video games. Cutting out all the blue light, the loud noise, and any excessive eye and brain stimulation will work wonders to calm down their little minds before sleep.

And try the Wi-Fi thing that we do in our house: put it on a timer. Every night it goes off around 11 p.m. or 12 a.m. and then comes back up at 7 a.m. Try doing the same thing with your Wi-Fi during sleep hours and see how that helps *all* of you get a better night's sleep.

And if you allow your child a cellphone, even though they're not yet in their teens, that's your business, but please, for the love of God, do not let them sleep with their cellular devices in their bedrooms, next to their heads. I mean, honestly. In Chapter Two, I talked about electromagnetic radiation. Yannick and I don't keep our iPhones in our bedroom, although all of our girls do, much to my disappointment. On rare occasions, when we're away from home and don't have our battery-operated alarm clocks with us so we need to use our phones as our alarms, they are always on airplane mode. At least our youngest is aware of the possible dangers and is diligent about keeping her iPhone on airplane mode during sleep. (So much so, that when she was in Paris during the attacks back in November 2015, we couldn't find her for more than two hours. We called her cell what felt like a million times, but it kept going to straight to voicemail. Each time it did, we all died a little more inside. Luckily, even though she was only a mile from the café attacks, she was safe. She and all her friends had been fast asleep. Her friends who didn't have their phones on airplane mode were alerted by their parents and shared the news of the attacks with Mikaela. When she finally called us, crying and shaken, we were all relieved that we, as a family, got good news that night, while so many others did not. I'll be honest with you — it was the only time in her life that I ever wished she'd disobeyed something we had impressed on her for years.)

Good old exercise helps regulate our bodies and improves our overall energy, but digital technology is keeping us more and more sedentary. These days, children spend more time on devices than they do running around. Do yourself and your kid a favour and make sure they get exercise — whether through traditional outdoor playground fun or through something more organized. (You should get out there with them!)

> Something else that helps with sleep is ensuring your child is getting a good amount of exercise.

The last thing I will mention regarding getting everybody in your family sleeping is the family bed. I know I said do what works for you, and of course you should, but in my humble opinion, letting your kids sleep in your bed with you is a very bad idea. Remember what I said: if your marriage isn't your priority when your kids are little, it will produce problems down the line. Your relationship with your partner won't make it through the lack of one-to-one grown-up intimacy and connection that having a family bed creates. Every couple needs a sacred space — like their bed — that is solely theirs. Theirs in which to be together and alone. They need to be able to tumble into bed next to each other at the end of the day and decompress — even just to turn to each other and say, "WTF was today? God, I'm tired! Love you!" In this modern world, we're already fighting an uphill battle to remain connected to our partner throughout busy days and distracted evenings. We have to fight to really unplug. The temptation to stare at our phones or the television and just zone out is huge. We have so little available downtime left at the end of the day. Why would you hand your relationship more opportunity to be disconnected, and in bed? Is that what you signed up for at the beginning of your relationship?

Do you want to throw all sorts of obstacles at your partnership, then sit back and wait for it to come crashing down around you? No, I highly doubt that you do. The family bed thing is just one more obstacle to getting any precious alone time with your partner. I don't get it. I don't see the benefits of it. Unless you're planning on going to college with your kid, why bother? Put your relationship first! Your kids will thank you when you're still together, sitting on the same side of the wedding aisle together later on. So enough with the family bed, people. Get naked, get sleeping sans children, have sex, and stay together.

GET THE WHOLE FAMILY
EATING WELL

Another big issue that could be affecting your child's sleep habits and is important for so many other reasons as well: their eating habits. Listen, you'll never, ever get an argument out of me about making cooking easy for yourself. I abhor cooking dinner probably more than any other person on the planet. I know how much easier it is to order in, or pick up fast food on the way home, or whip up a yummy pasta. I get it. I'm with you. In a perfect world, this foodie girl would want every meal to be a delivery mechanism for butter or salt or both. Cooking healthy meals is not my idea of everyday fun. I want all food to be cozy comfort food. I don't naturally gravitate toward greens, salads, and lean proteins for meals. But I cook that way 'cos I know it's not only better for *me*, but it's also especially beneficial for my girls and my hubby. So, I work at it.

A key to a healthy, smart, and rested child is a good diet. Even on a budget, with proper, organized shopping, you can give your kids all the nutrients they need with fun, easy, economical meals. One of my girlfriends is a pastry chef, and she told me, "When grocery shopping, if you stick to all the outside aisles, you have a way better chance of maintaining a healthy weight and mental wellness." I hadn't thought about it until my friend who *bakes cakes for a living* pointed it out. Think about it. All the processed shit not only takes up the bulk of the

> A key to a healthy, smart, and rested child is a good diet.

store these days, but it's usually in the middle of every market, everywhere.

Try it for a little while. Shop only on the outside aisles of the store. This is where you'll find your fresh produce, your fish, your eggs, and your meat. And before you tell me that a $1.99 bag of pasta feeds more people than a $3.00 bunch of carrots, bear with me for one hot minute. There are studies proving that nutrient-rich foods not only give your body what it needs for health, focus, and good sleep, but fill you up and keep you full longer. Also, you can easily substitute a head of cauliflower for a bag of pasta. Seriously, go online; there are so many ways to use cauliflower as a substitute for rice or pasta, your head will spin. There is even cauliflower-crust pizza.

At first, it's not easy to make the switch, unless you're one of the lucky people who picked up this book of mine BBA. That means you've already turned around your eating habits to be super healthy. Yay, you! But if you're more like me, a lazy, disinterested cook, and your kid is closing in on those double digits, and you already have some pretty questionable feeding habits going on in your house, then take comfort in knowing that you can turn it around. Believe me — I know! I've been you. When I turned away from my middle-aisle shopping back in 2006, getting my family on board was like trying to turn a large ship on a dime. Each gave their strong, vocal opinions about this new thing in their lives called goat milk. Then came the protests against their new and improved packed lunches, as old favourites like yogourt tubes, cheese strings, and fruit roll-ups were replaced with cucumber slices, green-apple slices, salads with avocado dressing, and water. No more Capri Suns for them! Man oh man, it was rough. It took us almost an entire school year to transition. But before long, they started to say things like, "I had a piece of pizza and I seriously got so tired right after eating it, I wanted to nap!" Once they began noticing the health benefits of the switch we were all making, life, and grocery shopping, became much easier.

Take the time to learn how to feed your family well on a budget. We live in amazing times, my friends. We have access to so much information, and there are so many people just like us; people who have been through it and are willing to share their knowledge with us for *free*. Why not take advantage of it?

THE OVERUSE OF DISTRACTION DEVICES IN PARENTING

Stick with me. We're now halfway through the topics I want to address in this, our longest chapter together. Next up is the overuse of distraction devices in parenting. Seriously, what is going on out there? When my daughters, who are all first-generation device kids, comment that too many parents are allowing iPads, cellphones, and hand-held gaming devices when they're out dining, you know we have a problem! When young people in their twenties and thirties are noticing that more and more families are glued to their glowing blue screens, we're heading in the wrong direction. Just put the phones down, people. Honestly, life is so crammed, and there is so much that keeps us away from precious family time. For most families, just commuting to work eats up hours a day, every day. And most everywhere in the world, the cost of living is *so high* that we're putting in extra-long hours *at* that job — sometimes two jobs. All of this makes quality time with one another harder and harder to come by.

Listen, I get it. I'm exhausted at the end of my day, and I'm not even in the active, hands-on, all-day-long parenting mode like you are. I completely understand and empathize with you. I know just how valuable the few hours at the end of your day of downtime are. But believe me when I say this, in the way a good, long catch-up chat with your best bitch or bro can bring your shoulders down and rejuvenate you, drawing nearer to the little people you created can, too. That is why you had children, isn't it? To create a family? To have a bond with fellow human beings that will last you a lifetime? Or did you just want to hold a gender-reveal party?

I challenge all families who are guilty of the disconnected and distracted mealtime trend to put down your devices. Shut down the distractions. Take these precious moments. You have your family all gathered together over mealtimes. This is a golden, old-fashioned moment to talk with one another, catch up with each other, and hear what went on in each other's day. And for those of you who say "my kids won't" or "yeah, right, my partner will never go for that!" I have a suggestion. Wanna make it a fun family activity, to get everybody off their devices? Try putting your money where your mouth is, with the No-Device Meal Challenge.

> I challenge all families to put down your devices at mealtimes.

A great way to break the device addiction during meal-times is to play a little game. Make a family chart with everybody's name on it. For every mealtime your family members get through without picking up their devices, each member must put one dollar into the money jar. When the streak is broken, whomever breaks it gets an X on the chart; the money gets set aside and the jar is added to when the next mealtime goes without any device distraction. At the end of the month, the family member with the fewest device infractions wins the money out of the jar!

Don't email me and tell me that your family won't do this, that it is an impossible habit for your family to break. I don't buy it. Anyone who doesn't have a rule about a phone-, entertainment-, and gaming device–free mealtime should have more faith in the inherent nature of competition. Besides, who doesn't want some extra pocket change?

If you find that you're able to eat device free at home but fail miserably at it when you're out to eat, there are other strategies. Try these old-fashioned things I used to do (back when our kids were young and there was zero technology around). Bring little portable games along, the kind you can get at a dollar store, or probably on Amazon (those bastards sell everything!). Do they still make Etch A Sketch? If they do, get one! Bring a pad of paper to play Hangman, or X's and O's. Colouring books are amazing, and they still make them small enough to fit on a restaurant table. All of these antiquated ways of engaging and entertaining a kid can still be found easily. Wow. I can't believe I just typed "antiquated" when referencing my own kids' upbringing. Damn. That's crazy!

We also used to do this fun thing over mealtimes called the "high-low" game. We each took our turn sharing a highlight from our day, and a low point. This simple conversational game brought us closer to one another, and you can do it without buying a single thing. It also keeps the kids engaged in the social activity of being out together in a restaurant. Kids love to share about themselves, their days, their adventures, their interests. We're the ones who shut them down by not really listening to them when they attempt to open up to us. Handing them a device is a sure-fire way to make sure they stay inward focused. Draw them out by being genuinely interested in getting to know them.

While we're on the subject of good mealtime manners, let's address the parents who allow their children to run like wild animals through restaurants. Are you kidding me? Let's think about this for a moment and list the main reasons why this is so *not cool*: 1) It may not be your place of employment but it is a workplace for many other people, and if you wouldn't bring your kids to your own job and let them run around, let's not put others in this position. 2) It is a place where these employees often carry sharp objects, such as knives, and boiling hot items, like soup and coffee. Imagine your precious child slamming into these workers and any of these items landing on your precious "they can do anything" child? You would lose your parenting mind! So, let's not. 3) And last but not least and maybe even the most important point: every other person inside that establishment is using their hard-earned money for a lovely evening out, stress free from planning, preparing, and cleaning up after a meal. Don't let your entitled behaviour ruin dinner for others. Can I get an amen and a pinky swear from you that if you are guilty of this behaviour you will cease and desist immediately?

SET SCREEN-TIME LIMITS
THAT WORK FOR YOUR FAMILY

How much time *should* your kid(s) spend on devices, video games, and television? This will vary from family to family and depend on the child's age, their extracurricular activities, and their school workload. It will also have a great deal to do with your child's nature and what they can handle as far as stimulation. Whatever they are, you should have your own online safety practices and put limits on their "screen" time.

Yannick and I were old fashioned in the way we parented our girls. We really worked to get to know them, and to expand their minds through reading and conversation, even ensuring that we had dates and alone time with each of them every single week. We read to them a lot, had tons of puzzles around, and a good assortment of other toys that stimulated and encouraged their creativity. As for TV, we had a rule that each of them was allowed to pick one half-hour program a day, which they could watch after school. No television before school. We favoured leaving them to have extra sleep, and to sit down together to eat breakfast when schedules allowed, without any distractions — for them or us. We also never had a television on the main floor of our house when they were little; we had only one TV in the whole place. This made it easier to keep the thing off.

We did something similar when computers came along; we had just one and limited the time the kids got to spend on it. No zombie kids for us! Our computer was always in the kitchen, where we could watch what sites the girls were on and what they were doing. They were keenly aware that we were watching them. Our girls were never under any false understanding that they were in their own world while online. They knew that any moment of any day we could — and would — access their chats to see what the hell they were up to.

(Also, let's talk about violence for a sec. We were the sort of parents who were way more likely to take our girls to a romantic comedy when they were little than a Quentin Tarantino film. Maybe that sounds like a no-brainer to you, but isn't that basically what you're doing when you allow your kids to have unlimited access to video games? Let me just state for the record that I don't think we should let kids play violent video games — as opposed to the ones that help them learn to read and count — until they're thirteen, and even then there should be lots of discussion about the fact that it's all make believe: nobody really runs around shooting people and taking their cars. Well, they do, but you're not going to raise one of those people, now, are you?)

Listen, don't take it from me, a mom who happens to lean a little to the alarmist side when it comes to this stuff (Wi-Fi, cellphone usage, EMFs, and the notion that perhaps our governments aren't being as above board as they should be when it comes to the long-term effects; I mean, we all know about lobbyists, right?). I'm just saying look into it and gain your own convictions. Check out this excerpt from a 2018 article on CBS News:

> Children are spending way too much time in front of screens, says the American Heart Association, and it's urging parents to drastically cut the hours their kids are allowed to use their phones, computers, tablets, and video games.
>
> Kids and teens age 8 to 18 spend an average of more than seven hours a day looking at screens. The new warning from the AHA recommends parents limit screen time for kids to a maximum of just two hours per day. For younger children, age 2 to 5, the recommended limit is one hour per day.
>
> Research has linked screen time with an increased amount of sedentary behaviour in children and teens. While there is no long-term evidence yet to link screen time to an increased risk of health conditions like cardiovascular disease and high cholesterol, there is mounting evidence that it is associated with obesity, cardiologist and CBS News medical contributor Dr. Tara Narula explains.

How much screen time are you allowing your kids younger than ten every day? If it's up around seven hours, I'd say it's time to dial it *way back*. Put a book in front of their face instead. Or a puzzle, or do a craft together. I used to love crafting with my girls.

Now, keep in mind that for older teens, these numbers most likely include using computers for schoolwork. But for younger kids, we're talking about two to three hours each and every day, which doesn't sound bad until you do the math. Two to three hours per day is fourteen to twenty-one hours a week. Times that by a year and you've got a kid younger than ten who's spending 728 to 1,092 hours being a zombie person. That's 30.3 to 45.5 *days* lost to staring at a screen.

Time is the most precious resource any of us have: ask a parent who has just been told their child has cancer. Or a parent whose child is killed in a mass shooting.

Sorry for getting all heavy on you, but parents, we need to take back the time we're losing to excessive screen time. What I wouldn't give to go back in time and spend more quality time with my girls, and they didn't even have screens the way kids do today. The bottom line is that there are many good reasons not to let your kids live their lives in their rooms on their devices, but for me personally, the biggest reason is that it's time with them we can never get back.

> We need to take back the time we're losing to excessive screen time.

THINGS TO NIBBLE ON

A child acting out is simply a child calling out for structure, order, and discipline.

Set a solid example for your kids by fighting fair yourselves. No hitting below the belt with your words or actions. Be the person you want your child to be when they grow up.

Introduce the reality that sex is all around us. Don't treat it like something worthy of a big, formal sit-down talk. If you treat it like what it is — a natural, normal part of being a human — it will never be awkward for you, or them.

Sleep: make sure that they, and you, get it. If you're not getting it, talk to your doctor, or a naturopath who can help you achieve healthy sleep without medication.

A healthy diet will make every single aspect of your parenting life so much easier. Do a ninety-day challenge and then tell me you don't notice a huge difference in your sleeping, your brain function, and your kid's mood and energy levels.

Cut out the distraction devices during meals. Remember that you signed up to be a parent, right? Play games, talk, hang out — take the No-Device Meal Challenge. Have fun with it.

Decide what you and your parenting partner feel is a healthy amount of time for your kids to spend in front their computers, TV screens, cellphones, or tablets. Then implement that fixed timeline into their everyday lives.

Chapter Eight
Healthy Boundaries

YOU'VE NOW GOT A TON of wisdom about how to raise your young kid into a fabulous adult. You're an example to all your friends of how to discipline firmly and with love. You're teaching your kid to fight fair and setting the standard yourself. You're treating sex as a normal thing and letting your kid know they can talk to you about anything. You're focused on sleep, diet, and exercise, and you're limiting screen time. You have totally got this.

In this chapter, we'll tackle what I believe will be one of the toughest topics in your parenting journey: boundaries. This always freaks parents out. How much freedom is too much, and how much is not enough? I always parented with this in the back of my head: "They may be little, but they're still their own people, so treat them the way you want to be treated, and speak to them the way you want them to speak to you." It's really that simple.

We'll also discuss the art of not raising a bully or a racist, and letting them work things out with teachers, coaches, and other people in positions of authority over them. But first let's talk about your own boundaries with your kids.

How much freedom is too much, and how much is not enough?

SPYING ON YOUR KIDS IS *NOT* COOL

There's this new trend where some parents have installed nanny cams, in secret, inside their child's bedrooms.

I have this to say to you:

Hop off.

Good Lord, what are you all doing? Have you gone mad? Can you imagine if your parents had had a secret camera on you when you were young? The number of times they would have unwittingly caught you with your hands in your underwear, masturbating? Or practising your French-kissing skills on your pillow? Or humping your giant stuffed frog?

No humping your stuffed animals? That was just me? Shit. Well, that's awkward …

The bottom line for me on this topic is that everybody deserves their privacy. And you must understand this one important thing about being a parent: *you do not own your child.* Yes, you birthed them; yes, you house them and pay for them; and yes, you do all the things it takes to keep them alive, but that still doesn't give you ownership of your child. Period. End of story. Not negotiable. You must respect their individuality and their privacy. If you've done the work, if

156

you've raised them with strong morals and a healthy amount of respect for you and your house rules, then you really should have no reason to spy on them. And if you really are concerned about what they're doing on their cellphones, laptops, iPads, or whatever the hell you let them have in their bedrooms, why not do this instead: how about *not* allowing them to have them in their rooms at all? That's what we did. If they wanted to be on their devices — once laptops and cellphones became a part of our lives — they had to use them in common space. Also, at night when you fall into bed, if you're concerned you might have a light-footed bandit in your home who will go and get the devices and bring them into their bedroom, lock them up at night (the devices, I mean, not the children). But for the love of God, please do not spy on your children. It is such an invasion of privacy. There's a *huge difference* between wanting to keep your child safe from the seedy underbelly of online life and reading their chats with their friends, without their knowledge. Sometimes they'll want to tell their friends that you're an asshole, and they should be allowed to do that without repercussions. (I mean, after all, you've told your friends how much you dislike your kid from time to time.)

It's important to distinguish between doing something to keep them safe and acting in a way that shows a lack of trust toward your child. Try to engage them in genuine conversation about their day, their feelings, and how they behaved in the world today, while they were out of your sight, to find out more about them. Teach them how to be honest with all aspects of their lives, and to trust that you have the ability to listen to them without losing your mind on them when they share something that is less than "ideal behaviour." Do this for them and, believe me, there will be no need to spy on them.

There is only one instance where I advocate for searching their rooms and rooting through their belongings: if your Parent Spidey Senses tell you they are harming themselves. That's a completely acceptable time to sniff around to make sure they're safe and healthy. Ideally you wouldn't need to concern yourself with this until after the double digits, but from what I hear, the anxiety that can lead to self-harm is starting younger and younger. So are eating disorders. Don't assume these are "older-kid" issues. Pay attention, and stay alert. Most importantly, trust your gut! And should that gut instinct prove right, then open the dialogue right away. Often these issues are a cry for help. Get them the support they need to deal with anxiety and stress (which the increased usage of social media isn't helping with one bit).

If what your child is going through feels outside of your scope of "parent therapist" skills, get them help from somebody who specializes in the issue. It is never too early or too late to put a child in therapy. It doesn't mean there's anything wrong with your kid or you as a parent. Recognizing that you are out of your depth and that your kid is in trouble is brave and loving.

ONLINE SAFETY: YOU CAN NEVER BE TOO CAUTIOUS

Which leads us beautifully into online safety. I cannot stress this enough. The freaks and the creeps of the world are all online, and they're all hiding behind false identities, looking for kids to abuse. I'm not being dramatic — I'm speaking the truth. A girlfriend of mine just shared with me this awful story. A few years ago, a grown-ass, disgusting pig "man" was messaging her then nine-year-old, telling her she was "beautiful" and that he wanted her to shave his balls for him.

WTAF?

Say *what*?

Shocking, right? Disturbing, isn't it?

This is reality. There are just boatloads of seriously fucked-up people out there in the world. And no matter what social media sites tell you, there are no real filters that can keep them all out. None. You have to be so careful about what your kids are doing with their own social media. Even kids as young as seven or eight. Or, as above, nine. That is why I'm such an advocate for sharing social media profiles with your kids. You monitor what they're looking at, who they're talking to, and who is talking back to them. I mean, if you're going to allow them on platforms that specifically restrict accounts to kids aged thirteen (or even eighteen!) or older, and your kid is only nine, then the least you can do is spend time monitoring what they're seeing on there and what people are seeing of them.

> You have to be so careful about what your kids are doing with their own social media.

Another girlfriend told me about a group chat her daughter was on with a bunch of classmates. They were all ten years old. One of the boys took the chat in a sexually explicit direction, aimed at her daughter. Oh, yeah. A class-mate, getting sexual with his ten-year-old friend. Don't be surprised, folks; this has been going on forever, since long before social media. When I was in the sixth grade, a group of older boys that had behavioural and learning challenges in my public school attempted to rape me in my house. They had first gone to my best friend's house, but lucky for her, both her parents were home. Mine were not. Which would have got me raped by five boys if I hadn't had the sheer will and strength of my rage to fend them off.

I'm not sharing these stories with you to freak you out. I'm giving you the power of knowledge, so that you can be at the forefront of your child's safety. It is your primary job. After that, it's all about raising them to have their own know-ledge of how to be in the world. Be diligent, smart, and pro-active in their online and day-to-day safety. I always told my girls, "I'd rather be too safe and too diligent with your safety and have nothing happen to you than be too trusting and be sorry." They knew if they wanted to go to a sleepover, it could never be at a home I hadn't been to, and I needed to have met the parents first. I often opted to have the kids sleep at our place instead. As a sexual assault survivor — involving two people who were part of my family — I know all too well how two minutes can change the rest of a child's life.

I am telling you this because it informed what I wanted my daughters to understand about the world. I'm not going into detail here about this part of my personal his-tory, because it is a huge and important topic that deserves its own space. But I want to share this with you so you know that I don't pull any punches when it comes to the all-important issue of what young women, and men, need to know about their own safety.

I'd rather be overcautious and be proven wrong. That would mean that nothing happened to my girls and that perhaps my overzealousness was unwarranted. Far better that than to be super relaxed and casual and have any harm come to them.

I have another girlfriend whose then fourteen-year-old son had a passion and an eye for photography. He'd recently begun taking shots of Toronto, by the dozens. To promote himself, he started an Instagram account specifically to display his art. He also asked people to direct-message him to set up photo shoots. This could be a bad idea in the hands of the wrong kid, but his mom was an active partner in his endeavours. She followed him on his account, and made sure to delete any inappropriate comments, including profanity. She also talked with him about the dangers of strangers online. They had a very frank, open dialogue going on, and he knew he was not to go and meet anybody — under any circumstances, for any shoot — on his own. Anybody who wanted to connect with him on that level had to set it up through his mom, and she would always be in attendance.

That was vigilance. That was proactive. That was love.

Be like my girlfriend, and take every measure to safeguard your kid. But also, don't put them in a castle tower. It is a delicate balance, for sure. You need to safeguard and protect, but also give them the freedom they need to thrive, live, and learn. They still need to be kids and enjoy the freedoms that come with being little. A great resource on this topic is one of my all-time favourite books, *Protecting the Gift* by Gavin de Becker. It is an absolute must-read, with tons of practical ways to protect your child.

Believe me, there are a great many online predators. I work closely with an organization in Toronto called Boost for Kids, and one of the things we do is give counselling to kids who have been sexually abused online. It is a thing, guys. I know you aren't thinking about it right now, especially if your baby is still cooking in your oven, but it's real and it's important to be vigilant and have your mind made up early about what your rules are going to be.

You need to safeguard and protect, but also give them the freedom they need to thrive, live, and learn.

We also need to be aware of the toll that online living is taking on our children's mental wellness. Instagram believes this is real enough that they changed the way their platform works; your followers can no longer see how many likes you are or aren't getting. Okay, it's a small step, because the *subscriber* can still see whether or not the people following them give a shit. But I suppose small steps in the right direction are better than no steps at all. Studies have shown that frequent social media use by young kids and teens leads to increased stress and lower self-esteem. Kids get so busy trying to increase their number of followers or keep up with other people's ideal-looking lives that they can spiral into depression. As a mom who has gone through the fire of the preteen years times three, I can tell you that these emotions are already at the forefront of most preteens' brains as they struggle to find their identity, work through hormonal changes, and develop bonds of true friendship. Why allow them access to social media, which is only going to add fuel to this fire, when they're already so vulnerable?

Had all this stuff existed when our girls were little, it would have been an easy decision ... it would have been a *no* from me, at least until my girls were in a more emotionally stable frame of mind, where their self-esteem wasn't so fragile and they weren't so susceptible to feeling left out. This time will be different for every kid; some may be totally cool in their own skin by the time they're twelve, some may be fifteen, and for others, it may take until they're twenty-one. Our personalities are as unique as our fingerprints, and as parents it's our job to know our kids and guide them accordingly. Let's not throw them into the lion's den prematurely. Use your better judgment and give your kid privileges to the online world based on their ability to handle it. I mean, for Christ's sake, I don't know how you all feel, but there are times that I myself have to take a break from social media. As a natural type-A, competitive person, watching other people "breeze" through life and have career victory after career victory has sometimes made me question my worth. And I'm a grown-ass, pretty incredible woman, if I do say so myself! I'm sure you can point to instances where it hasn't had such a great effect on you, either. So if it can rattle *us,* just imagine what it can do to young, impressionable kids.

DON'T USE YOUR KIDS TO BOOST YOUR SOCIAL MEDIA PROFILE

All right, Mom and Dad, I'm going to get a bit tough on you right now. Remember when I said that our kids don't belong to us, that we don't "own" them? Yeah, well, that's especially true when it comes to us adults on social media. Our children's struggles are theirs and theirs alone. They are private, difficult moments in their lives, not yours to share. I point this out because I once saw a video of a young girl, probably about six, having a meltdown. She was so genuinely upset over something that she was convulsing. And what did the dad do? Did he console her? Did he draw her close and comfort her, in what was clearly a time of need in her young life? No. No, he did not. He videotaped it and put it on social media. And the worst thing possible happened to his dumb-ass video: it went viral. His daughter was too young to have her own social media accounts or even to have a voice in what would or would not be posted about her. And there she was on full display in a most vulnerable moment, betrayed by one of the people who should make her feel the safest. It broke my heart. And sadly, her dad is not alone. Parents post videos all damn day of their kids coming off anesthesia, having been afraid of having a tooth pulled. You name it, if a child is in a vulnerable state but happens to do something "funny," and the parent thinks it might get some likes and give them their fifteen minutes of social media fame, you bet your ass that video is going online. All without the consent of the child.

Gross.

The most famous case of an over-sharer looking for online fame is Christie Tate and her daughter, who, once she was old enough to go online, found that her entire life — all her embarrassing, awkward, private moments — had been on display since the day she was born. Can you imagine? I mean, think about it for a second. How would you feel if you came to learn that somebody you were in an intimate relationship with had a blog and had documented every single moment of your life, not only without your consent, but without your knowledge? Just sit with that question for a moment.

> Respect your child's right to privacy, even when they're too little to ask you not to post about them.

You wouldn't like it, would you?

So then why would you think your child would like it?

These are parents who have lost their cool.

Don't be one of these parents. Respect your child's right to privacy, even when they're too little to ask you not to post about them ... *especially* when they're too little. It's your job to protect them and keep their lives private.

We don't own them.

Even now, with my girls being grown-up women with their own social media profiles, I still ask them if it's okay to share a photo, or a work victory, or anything at all about them, online. Often, they say no. In fact, they've even asked me to delete Instagram captions, saying they were too pointed and private.

You know what I did? I listened to them and respected their boundaries.

SHANTELLE BISSON

Do the same. It's powerfully bonding and builds a depth of trust that will not easily be broken.

I'm not saying don't post family vacay photos, or cute videos of them dancing around the house, or anything that shows them in a positive light. That's cute, and it is nice to see happy children on the internet. I'm telling you not to *exploit* them for your own popularity.

DON'T RAISE A BULLY

A big safety issue is bullying, which, of course, happens both in person and online. This is such a huge subject that it requires an entirely separate discussion; I just might write a book on that topic alone. All three of my girls were bullied; I was bullied; hell, I'm sure even you were bullied. It really is a universal experience that we can all relate to. The one thing I will say on this subject is if your child is being bullied or teased, go right to the source. Ask the principal of your school to call a meeting with the other child and their parents. Do not allow bullying to go unchallenged. No matter what.

Another benefit to limiting screen time is that it is a great way to protect your kid from any unpleasantness that might follow them home from school. When I was young, there were no cellphones, no computers, nothing. That meant if you were being bullied at school, it ended at 3:30 p.m. When you got home, you were home, in the cocoon of your family. You had a completely safe place away from it all. Nowadays, if your child is dealing with bullies at school, those kids literally have access

166

to them all day long via their social media platforms, through texting, and on and on. Limiting their time on their devices once they're home is a form of protection, not punishment. Keep that in mind when they're crying for more time.

And parents, make sure that your kid is not the one doing the bullying. If they are, then do what we did when one of our girls tried being a bully for a short time: take away their privileges and have serious discussions with them about the pain they're causing the other person. Make it real for them by sharing any bullying experiences you may have endured, to help them understand how painful it is and how it can damage a person well into adulthood. Check with their teacher about your child's schoolyard behaviour. Nip it in the bud by being an active participant in raising a decent member of society. That includes teaching them tolerance for those who are different from them, whether in skin colour, religious background, socioeconomic circumstances, sexual orientation, or something else. None of these differences are a reason for your child to treat kids any differently from the kids who look and live like them.

Racism and bullying can begin, but can also end, at home. It is up to every single one of us to lead with love. To teach our children to treat everybody with love. As corny as it sounds, I believe we have the power to create the world as we want it to be: a world where everybody is treated with kindness and acceptance. After all, regardless of the colour of our skin, what our job or status is, who we love, or what gender we identify with, we all leave this earth the same way: naked and on our own. As my mother always said, "Nobody is more special than anybody else; we all put our pants on one leg at a time."

She would say this to me to encourage me to believe in myself, to believe that I too could become more than my circumstances, that the fact that we were poor should never keep me from trying. It's more important now than ever that we teach our children acceptance. Kids as young as nine have committed suicide as a result of bullying. We need to do better. We must do better. No parent should have to join the club of parents whose child takes their own life because they can see no other way. So, how about don't be a bully to your kids, and your kids won't grow into bullies. Let's start there.

TRUSTING YOUR GUT AND BEING AWARE

Another part of protecting your child is keeping an eye on coaches and other people who have access to your kids during their after-school activities. It's stunning just how often harm comes to a child from people in such roles. Of course, you can't let this fear keep your child from getting out there and finding their passion. Like every aspect of parenting, you just need to be alert and aware. Trust your instincts. Teach your children how to safeguard themselves when they're out in the world. This is the time when putting down the distraction devices and getting close to your child will prove invaluable. You need to develop a deep sense of trust between you and your kid, so they know they can come to

THINGS TO NIBBLE ON

We do not, ever, need to install secret cameras in our kids' bedrooms. N.E.V.E.R. It is a gross misuse of power, and an invasion of privacy.

I cannot stress how important online safety is. If you allow your child to be on devices, and if you allow them to have social media accounts, please, I'm begging you, be diligent. Protect the gift, protect the gift, protect the gift.

If you want to be cool, don't use your kids' child-hoods to boost your online social media presence. Another huge invasion of their privacy.

Let your kid fight their own battles and learn how to resolve conflicts with people in positions of author-ity, such as their teachers. Keep your cool by not doing their school projects and fighting for better grades on their behalf.

Trust your gut. It is always better to err on the side of caution by not allowing somebody in your child's life than it is to think you're being silly, only to find out that you actually weren't.

Don't be a bully, so you don't raise a bully. Treat every other human being with the dignity they deserve. Make sure you raise a person who goes out into the world and leads with love.

Look at how awesome you are. You're a badass, rock-star parent, so put down this book and go have sex!

you with anything. You need to know that a stranger, or opportunistic sicko, can't convince your child it's better to keep a secret from you than to tell you. Be your kids' safe place. Make sure they know how deeply invested you are in every aspect of them. Ensure you are connected with them through regular conversation. The more you talk with your kid, the more you will learn and understand them.

Now go have sex. Happy, satisfied people make better humans.

Chapter Nine

Over-Programming and the Art of Boredom

YOU'RE COMMITTED TO GIVING your kids their privacy, but also monitoring their online activities and trusting your gut when something doesn't feel right. You're keeping your cool by not posting online every embarrassing thing your kid ever does. And most of all, you're teaching your kid about respect and leading with love. You're pretty much a parenting master at this point. But there's more.

I've left this chapter to near the end for a reason: I'm deeply passionate about this topic. In our modern society, where everybody is "go, go, go" all the time, it seems that relaxation and boredom are dying arts. But I'm here to tell you it's an old-fashioned pastime that we *must* bring back in order to enjoy a balanced, healthy, and *long* life. I've said it before, and I'll say it again: I'm no doctor. I'm also not a researcher, so I won't give you cold, hard facts on this topic.

But I can share something I've learned from many doctors who have cared for me over the years, and that is that stress raises cortisol levels, and raised cortisol levels keep us from getting proper, deep rest. Raised cortisol levels also make us fat. How does "overweight and exhausted" sound? Neither are conducive to a healthy lifestyle. Stress weakens our immune system, and weakened immune systems lead to illness. And let's face it, stress stresses us out! So, knowing all these facts, and knowing you love your kids, why would you over-program them to the point of stressing them out? Why would you stress out your kids, thus raising their risk of illness and obesity?

The short answer is I know you don't want to do these things. This chapter is going to help you stop doing that.

In order to be good parents, you must fill and refill your own fuel tank, ensuring that you feel rock solid and centred.

Along with the health and wellness benefits for your kid, slowing down and stopping the over-programming will also benefit your own sanity.

Our modern world moves at warp speed. Everything is fast, faster, fastest. We want everything yesterday, and we don't want to get out of our cars to get it. We're so addicted to speed and convenience that we now have a drive-through for almost everything. There are drive-through bank machines, coffee shops, dry cleaners and, of course, the ever-present drive-through for food! With our over-programmed, stuffed-to-the-brim-with-shit-to-do lifestyle, we have forced the world to speed up with us. We can grab virtually anything and everything while on the go. Our kids spend more time eating in cars on their way to this activity or that than they do at the family table. It's insane. And it needs to stop.

In bestselling author Carl Honoré's book *In Praise of Slow*, he coined a term that really struck me: "slow parenting." Without even knowing that we were doing it, Yannick and I had always practised slow parenting with our girls. We weren't the sort of parents who allowed or forced our children into multiple activities. This was in part because we selfishly wanted our *own* downtime. We didn't want our lives to revolve around them and their whims and interests. In order to be good parents, you must fill and refill your own fuel tank, ensuring that you feel rock solid and centred. If you don't, it's far too easy for your heart to fill with bitterness over the fact that you have no time for yourself. Selfishness is not a bad thing for a parent; you need a healthy amount of it to be your best you. When you are your best self, then guess what happens? You feel stronger and more positive in your own life and you're going to raise much better people.

Lots of parents pack their kids' lives with activities because they're afraid that otherwise they'll raise some sort of noodle, a person who can't "compete" in some way, or a kid who doesn't get good enough grades because they're not in endless Kumon lessons and other tutoring. The truth, in fact, is quite the opposite. When a child is raised to know that having some open time on their hands is a very, very good thing, they learn some valuable lessons. They learn to be content in themselves, and they learn how to combat boredom. They learn how to create their own happiness. They learn how to unwind, relax, and listen to their own souls. How many adults do you know who could learn from this simple philosophy? By slowing down, we all get the opportunity to spend more time with ourselves — a kind of natural meditation, if you will. When a child is faced with nothing to do, and nowhere to go, they have to *be* with themselves. This is where creativity thrives and problem-solving abounds.

When our girls were younger, we had tons of puzzles, colouring books, dolls, costumes, you name it. When birthdays rolled around, we told family and friends to give them crafty gifts — things that encouraged them to use their creativity. A child's mind is a wondrous, pure, and imaginative space. Take away some of those over-programmed and hyper-organized activities that you've been bamboozled into thinking are "good for your child" and provide some easy-going, open-ended time for your kid. Let them discover how much good is already inside them. Let them settle into their own mental space a bit, and teach them that it's okay to have downtime. The problem with over-programming is that you're inhibiting your child's ability to uncover the world at their own pace and see it through their own eyes. Instead, as they get shuttled from one activity to another, they are constantly bombarded with what somebody else thinks, feels, and believes. Letting your child discover for themselves the magic of time and stillness is one of the most incredible gifts you can give them. And by doing so, you'll end up with some extra time to do the exact same thing for yourself. Do this in tandem with your child and watch both your lives open up.

Our financial situation forced us into this "slow-parenting" method long before Honoré wrote about it. It turned out beautifully, and truth be told, I don't regret having been able to give them only one after-school activity each. What I see now is parents running themselves into an early grave by criss-crossing the city — and in some cases, the country — to make sure their children *have it all*. It looks like madness. It is madness. I mean, honestly, I'm exhausted watching you all. How do you have any time or energy ... for sex? Seriously. Slow down. Because what good is having it all if you lose yourself? I'm asking you this for your own sake, but also for the sake of your kid. You and I both know the answer: it is no good *at all*.

I do think it's important for the healthy development of your child that they participate in at least one activity. But people, you must find balance. Carl's books, *In Praise of Slow* and his equally wonderful book *Under Pressure*, are must-reads. They're wonderful books to read alongside this one. I strongly recommend them both. They will give you the boost of confidence you're going to need when you get that sideways look on the playground, or when you're volunteering on that class trip, and all the high-pressure yummy mummies turn their noses up at you for *not* programming your kid to death. You will have me and Carl in your back pocket. You will know that slowing down, as well as cultivating the art of boredom, are much, much better for your kid's long-term health than running them ragged.

Just look at how it turned out for us. All three of our girls are able to spend hours and hours *alone* without freaking out. They don't feel anxious that they're "missing out" or that they're "wasting time." They crave downtime and look forward to the days in their schedules where they have the freedom to be "bored." We had no idea that our lack of money would give them such a gift.

This is a delicate dance, though. Don't use the idea of slow parenting as an excuse to be a lazy parent, or to spend more time sitting around in your PJs on social media, or binge-watching your favourite television shows. I'm not giving you permission to go home at the end of every day to whip off your bra and get into comfy, cozy mode and let things slip. You still need to keep your kids involved in something outside the four walls of your family home. A great way to do that is get them involved with volunteering. Yannick and I became quite philanthropic thanks to our youngest daughter, who, when she was fourteen, started making bracelets for kids fighting cancer at SickKids in Toronto. It was because of her charity work and her pure heart that we were inspired to do more for those around us. It's a wonderful way to teach your kids gratitude and empathy. Developing all the sides of your child makes for better humans.

> Slow down and cultivate the art of boredom.

Now, before you get all pissed off at me, saying, "You said to not have them doing too many things — now you're telling me to get them involved in charity work," well, yes, I am. Doing something they're passionate about and that's good for their community is good for their self-esteem and good for their souls. I'm helping you raise a well-rounded, multi-dimensional human being.

You're welcome.

LET THEM FOCUS ON THEIR PASSION

Even when our girls wanted to do absolutely nothing, Yannick and I insisted they do something they were passionate about. Every child needs to be engaged in at least one activity that helps to build their self-esteem, self-confidence, self-worth, and independence — not only independence from you, but from any siblings they might have. When our girls were little, we let them dip their toes in many pools so they could discover their natural talents and passions. I began dancing when I was four, and Yannick began skiing when he was two. We loved doing those things, and throughout our lives they have remained top passions. Some kids will lead you right to theirs, while others might shift interest and direction many times over the course of their young lives. Others might not have the foggiest idea what they like, or what they want to pursue. That's when trying out many different extracurricular activities comes in super handy (and no, I don't mean all at once! We're not overloading them, remember? Try things one at a time). The most important thing as a parent is to help them find something to participate in that encourages confidence-building, team-building skills, discipline (there's that word again), and the art of losing. This last one is imperative to their healthy development. It teaches them to be corrected, and to lose sometimes without crumbling. Also, I suggest that you be the parent who says you don't want your kids to get a ribbon or trophy "just for showing up." I'd love it if you spearheaded the trend of kids learning about losing and winning, and how to handle both. There are winners and losers in all sports, and that's really okay. In the real world, they might get an F on a paper. They might not make a team in high school. Hell, perhaps like you, they might never see their favourite sports team win a championship in their lifetime. And they sure as shit are not getting the first job they ever apply for. Help them out now by teaching them how to deal with failure. Part of that also means teaching them how to thrive when faced with failure.

> Help them find something to participate in that encourages confidence-building, team-building skills, discipline, and the art of losing.

Help them to understand that we can learn from our failures and trust that things will always be all right in the end, and if things aren't all right, then it isn't the end. Failure is not just about getting knocked down — it's about what you do after you're knocked down. It's about learning how you get up again and take that lesson forward in positive and galvanizing ways.

If your kid ends up falling in love with a sport, that's amazing, as sports help keep them healthy and active. Sports also teach them teamwork skills, the art of getting along with varying personalities, and how to lose. If you end up with a child who is obsessed with the arts — dance, music, drawing — know that these activities enrich their minds. No matter what kind of artistic experience your child picks, they are all win-win options. Even if they don't end up pursuing that artistic passion professionally (and chances are, they won't), it will provide them with pleasure and interests for the rest of their lives. The key to helping your kid find their passion is to talk to them, observe them, figure out what they naturally gravitate to, and then help them find the way to make that passion a reality.

If you find yourselves, like Yannick and I did when our kids were little, tight for cash, then look for free local options. Many community centres offer free or low-cost after-school programs. Or you can get creative and join a non-denominational church in your community that offers free activities for kids. Enlist the help of grandparents to cover some of the cost of the activity instead of throwing presents at them at every occasion. Be the one who starts a drawing group for your kid and their friends; be the parent who takes them all to the library. Start a Mommy and Kid reading group. Ask your village around you for ideas. Every child should participate in one soul-enriching activity. And to the parents who claim to have a "lazy" or "uninterested" child, to that I say there is no such thing! You simply haven't found what sparks their joy. For the longest time, our middle girl didn't want to try anything, and she hated *everything* she did try. We were *this close* to giving up. She was seven. She had tried ballet, gymnastics, figure skating, art classes, tap, jazz, baseball, soccer … you name it, we put her in it. And she hated every single activity. Getting her to go was like pulling teeth. But in our house, everybody had to try an activity until they found the one that ignited their passion. We knew they could learn vital life skills that only these sorts of activities can teach them. Then, fate intervened and we moved back to Toronto, while Yannick filmed a Canadian series. As luck would have it, we moved ten minutes from a horseback-riding school in the heart of Toronto. She took to it like a moth to a flame. We had done it: she *loved* something, at long last. Our perseverance had paid off for her, and us.

She excelled at it, too. I can't tell you the confidence boost it gave her, and the pride she walked with after finding something that was all hers, that she was good at. It was like night and day. Even to this day, twenty years later, she still gets up on a horse and finds her happy place.

Each and every kid has that thing inside them. Don't quit until you help them uncover it. The payoff of watching them live out a passion is like nothing else you will witness. Also, having an outside person in their lives, like a coach or an instructor, calling them on their shit, pushing them to not quit, is so important. They need to hear that kind of thing from someone they respect who isn't their parent. They need to hear someone push them to master that footwork, or take ten more shots at the net. A great coach or instructor can be instrumental in a kid's life. Having discipline enforced by another adult can go much farther than when it just comes from you. When a coach says "there's always another game" when they lose, or pushes them to "try that move *one more time*," they hear it. And it takes some of that pressure off you to always be that voice. That too is a very good thing.

In addition to helping them find that one thing, while we were always careful not to over-program them, we also made all of them participate in a self-defence form of exercise. We insisted on the self-defence element because one in three girls and one in five boys will be sexually assaulted in their lifetimes. That's the statistic. We wanted to give them the confidence that comes with being a young woman who knows how to kick ass. We wanted them to feel strong and walk with their shoulders squared and their heads high. And should that not be sufficient, we wanted to ensure that they had tools to fend off an attacker, should it (please God, *never*) get that far. Now that they all live on their own, knowing they have this skill helps us sleep better at night. This is why I strongly suggest you get your children involved in some kind of self-defence class.

But that's it. One passion, one self-defence class.

Honestly, this trend of believing that the more your kid does, the better it is for them is driving *everybody* crazy. Most specifically, it's driving the kids crazy. It doesn't reflect badly on your parenting if your child has one day on which they don't have an extracurricular activity after school. Kids love being home. They love being around their things, or playing outside with neighbour kids, relaxing on their beds, reading, colouring, or just doing nothing. My girls loved nothing more than sleeping in on the weekends, staying in their PJs as long as they wanted to, and having family breakfast at noon all together. It was heavenly, and it felt decadent. *Slow down.* Just be together with nowhere to be and nothing pressing to do. Being at home with nothing to do takes us all back to simpler times — times of peace, pleasure, and comfort. How can any of us ever have too much of that?

Kids don't want to be operating at a million miles an hour. They also don't want to be eating McDonald's or Subway in the back seat of your car day after day after day. This is why I believe that one passion program, and one self-defence program, along with school five days a week, homework, and chores is plenty.

START CHORES AS YOUNG AS POSSIBLE

Ahhh, chores. Yes. This was a given, wasn't it? Didn't you and your partner decide that you brought this little person into your world to make your life a bit easier? No? Well, part of having kids is that they get to pick up some of the day-in-day-out shit that it takes to run a house. Now, I'm even talking about little kids. If they can play with Play-Doh, they can put the Play-Doh away. Same goes with their arts and crafts supplies, their dolls, their costumes, what have you. Yes, Virginia, a two-year-old sure as hell can put all those toys back in the toy bin when they're done playing. And as they get older, they should start to do things like make their beds, help with the dishes, and set and clear the family meal table. Do yourself a favour and start teaching them the importance of being a team player in the upkeep of the house when they are small. When they are little, they will enjoy it — after all, they get to spend time with you doing the things you do in the house. Then it will become second nature to them, for which their future life partners will thank you! You're teaching them responsibility for themselves and their surroundings, and how to carry their own weight in a household. You are teaching them that they are part of a family, and every member of a family is responsible to every other member. This includes keeping the household operating. Plus, it makes them better roommates, too!

THE MANY BENEFITS OF BOREDOM

Something else beautiful comes out of not programming the snot out of your kid: you will recover much needed one-on-one time with your child. If you and your kid both have free time, you will discover the joy of being able to have weekly dates with each other. You will have time to let your child pick an activity they want to do with you, and then just go and do it together. This means you, too, dads. Kids are not used to getting their father's attention all to themselves. Honestly, our girls looked forward more to their dates with Yannick than with me. Not because they loved me less, but because often kids are just used to being with their mothers more than their fathers. So, dads, make this a priority. Both parents should set aside a few hours each week to go and have some alone time with your kid. You will get to know them on a more intimate level and you'll solidify your relationship with one another. I cannot stress enough the importance of this. It will repay you in ways you can't imagine. Just do this one thing. The payoff is truly priceless.

Let them be bored. I will repeat this. For God's sake, let them be bored! Incredible things can be created out of boredom. Boredom teaches them how to be alone, and still thrive. In addition to helping them learn to be content by themselves, it will help them be able to walk away from unhealthy relationships when they're older. They will have the sure and strong knowledge that being alone isn't a scary thing — it's nurturing and wonderful. Boredom will allow them to tune into themselves. It will help them decode the things that make them feel bored, too. They will be able to figure out when boredom is uncomfortable for them, when it is an opportunity for self-discovery, and when it is simply a way to decompress their busy brains. This is something they can't do if they're constantly running around.

Besides, let's be honest with one another. After a particularly gruelling schedule of your own, when you've had to work overtime and been caught in traffic, when it seems as if you haven't put your feet up in *forever*, how awesome does it feel to just do nothing? You and I have both been there. There is no better feeling in the world than knowing you have nothing on your schedule the next day. If you feel this way, imagine how much your child craves this same gift.

Besides, think of how badass and cool you'll be on the playground! You'll be the one all the other parents are talking about. "Did you know that so and so has her kid in only *one* activity?" Which you and I both know they're secretly jealous of, because, let's be frank, if you're not constantly running around with your kid, think of all the hot sex you're having! You know it, I know it, and they know it, too.

So, fly my little parent birds! Lighten up, slow down, and have sex!

THINGS TO NIBBLE ON

Slow down. It's not only good for your health and your soul, but also your kid's.

Help them find their passion, whether through volunteering, arts, sports, or whatever it might be. When a kid has even one thing that lifts their spirit and their confidence, their faith in their ability to achieve will soar.

Have them start chores when they're little, so that when they go out into the world, they will know how to maintain their own household. Their future partner thanks you.

The benefits of allowing your child to experience boredom far outweigh the benefits of programming them to death. And honestly, who even cares about how it benefits them; think about all the extra time *you're* going to have to do things you want to do, or even just to do nothing.

Look at you! You're having a blast with the small humans living in your home, and you're feeling confident! And confidence makes you feel sexy …

So, go have sex!

Chapter Ten

Mommy Madness

THROUGHOUT THIS BOOK, I have tried to inspire you and give you lots of food for thought about how to raise a free but respectful, unentitled child. My goal was to be as truthful as possible with you, to really prepare you for what's ahead.

I didn't write this book because I went through my entire parenting journey without losing my cool. I wrote this book because despite how often I actually *did* lose my cool, somehow my girls turned out awesome. I didn't write this book to rub it in anybody's face about how incredible my girls are now, as if it was effortless, and how I'd done the best, most perfect job of mothering ever.

This book came out of my utter astonishment that in spite of myself, I somehow ended up with these three wonderful, thoughtful, conscientious adults. I made them.

They turned out more than okay, and — being completely transparent here — that happened despite all the ways I fucked up. I fucked up weekly, for certain, and some weeks, like before my period, it may have been daily. Hell, it may have even been hourly.

There were way too many times where I said something rash and harsh because of something else that was weighing on me, something that had literally nothing at all to do with my kids. Yet they were closest to me in the moment and took the brunt of my upset.

Many nights, I cried myself to sleep once the house was quiet, with Yannick sleeping soundly next to me, because I was completely and utterly out of my depth. I can't even count the number of times that I was sure with every fibre in my being that I had fucked up beyond repair, that despite all my efforts to do better than my mom (and don't we all, even if we love and respect our parents, have some things that we don't want to repeat?), I thought not only was I not doing better, but I was actually failing at it.

I wrote this book because when you're lost, overwhelmed, and afraid during your parenting journey, the tips in this book will save you. They will help you create incredible human beings. The advice I've put in these pages are the things I did consistently, that I managed to hold on to even when I was a complete and utter mess. I stuck to these golden nuggets, and my girls all came out of it okay.

So, don't worry. Stop beating yourselves up. We moms, especially, are so very good at that. But don't. You're not alone. Almost every other parent out there has stood in front of a mirror with Louis-Vuitton-suitcase-sized bags under their eyes and confidently told themselves, "I can't do this."

But you can. I'm here to tell you that if I can, you can. But you have to take care of yourself. You have to extract yourself from the madness on a regular basis to get back to you, so that you can be the best version of yourself. Take some time away, entirely on your own, with a friend or with your partner. It's the key to making it through the trying times. Trust me: doing this saved me.

I cannot stress enough how important it is to take it easy on yourself when you completely and utterly blow it, like when they're little and they've been crying for the better part of twenty-four hours for weeks on end, and you're begging and pleading with your baby to just *stop*. When you're screaming louder than they are, and tears are streaming down both of your faces. Lost. Helpless. Scared.

That was me. Often.

It's not easy, and hopefully none of your friends said it was going to be easy — although everything you've been seeing on Instagram for years probably has you convinced that for some it's not only easy, it's downright fucking perfect. I'm here to tell you that it is not. Take it from somebody who has done it *three times*. It is not easy. Oh, sure, there are moments that may last hours, or even carry on for days, weeks, or months, where everything is humming along nicely. You and your partner are doing beautifully, getting along, having plenty of sex, going on dates, fully and completely connected. The kids are sleeping well, eating well, and haven't had lice or the flu in the last minute or so. All this will cause you to totally forget how much it hurt to push their tiny human bodies out of your vag or how downright terrible their last meltdown was. Life is blissful and calm. But is it perfect? No. It's not. Because there is no such thing as perfect. Therefore, there is no reason for you to compare your parenting journey to anybody else's, especially one you see on the internet. Don't fall into that trap. Trust yourself more. Protect yourself more. As long as you wake up every single day of your life committed to doing your best for your child(ren), there is no way you won't. Your best is yours. Somebody else's is theirs. And if it weren't for the internet, nobody would give a damn about pitting themselves and their kids against the progress, or lack thereof, of somebody else.

Do yourself a favour and put down the phone.

Take time to develop your own parenting rhythm that works for you and your baby. Listen to your own intuition because, after all, you're pretty fucking cool — always have been. Don't forget that.

> There is no reason for you to compare your parenting journey to anybody else's, especially one you see on the internet.

The one thing I did — and still do — when I know I'm about to boil over, which has saved me from going past the point of no return, is to remove myself from the situation. When the girls were little, especially Brianna, after totally and completely losing my cool one too many times, I decided that rather than scream at an innocent baby, I would just lay her down in her crib and get as far away from her as I could get while not leaving the house. For me, that was our unfinished basement (totally glamorous, I know). And that's where I would stay until I'd yelled, cried, and sometimes pulled my hair out enough to get back to my centre.

Maybe you won't ever explode like this. I hope you don't. It's an awful, downright devastating feeling. But you have to forgive yourself if you do. Apologize to yourself for letting yourself down. This is what I did every time I fell, each time I believed I couldn't go on and was convinced that I was by far the absolute worst parent who ever walked the earth. I would pull myself together and get back in the battle.

And therein lies the ultimate secret to successful parenting. As long as you always get back in the fight of trying to raise the best human you can, then you will. Because, remember, you're awesome, and you've got this!

FINAL NIBBLES

Raising your kids will bring you all the joy in the world *if* you're prepared, and *if* you know going in that it is the single most difficult job you will ever take on, and *if* you don't go into it blindly expecting perfection from yourself, your partner, and your kids. The bottom line is that life is messy, and tough, and often scary. But it is also beautiful, remarkable, wonderful, and rewarding. Go into your parenting prepared, just as you would go into battle. I promise you will end up with well-adjusted adults you want to spend your time with, and a partner you can spend the rest of your life with. You will all be happily intertwined as a *family*, and you will be able to build a rich and beautiful family life.

Keep these few key things in mind and you will be the envy of your friends who didn't buy my book and use my easy-to-follow methods for parenting while keeping their own "cool" intact.

The world won't come to them on a silver platter, so don't send them out into the world believing that it will.

1) Don't take any of it too seriously. You're not the first people to procreate, and you won't be the last. Your child is much more resilient than you know or give them credit for; don't coddle them. Overprotection won't do them any favours when they eventually leave your nest and go out into this giant world of ours. If you've been paying attention, you are all too aware that the world isn't getting any kinder at the moment. You need to prepare your child for *real life*, not life in the cozy bubble of your home where your kid is treated like the most awesome, wonderful, brilliant human to walk the earth. Now, I'm not telling you that you shouldn't be your kid's biggest fan, that you should hang them out to dry and leave them on their own to "sort it all out." Not at all. I'm reminding you that you need to parent them with balance. Be tough on them when they need you to be tough on them. Tell them *no*. Don't try to be their best friend and favourite person. That will get neither of you anywhere fast. Don't let your child get a ribbon for "showing up." Teach them that hard work equals reward. The world won't come to

them on a silver platter, so don't send them out into the world believing that it will.

2) Be humble. Practise humility with your kids and your partner. Admit when you fuck up. You're human. You're probably going to do it a lot, so *own it*. By owning your bullshit and your meltdowns or overreactions, you'll show your kids how to deal with people outside your family when they melt down or blow up. It also teaches them something even more valuable, and a mindset that is sadly dying out in our modern society: it's not a sign of weakness to apologize when you're wrong. Life isn't about being right, or winning an argument. You're teaching them that, in fact, it's the complete opposite. Life is better lived if it's done with love and humility. It takes great strength to look somebody dead in the eye, take that deep breath of courage and utter the words *I am sorry*. In doing this, you teach them about letting go, about forgiveness, and about how absolutely amazing it feels to be apologized to. Kids respond to humility, and often, if they're like mine, they will throw their tiny little arms around you and tell you that they love you, and that it's okay. And when they go out into the world and have relationships with all kinds of people, they will show others how powerful an apology can be.

3) Your kids will grow up and leave, so contrary to popular belief, they are not your most important relationship in your family. After making sure that you never stop working on bettering yourself,

feeding your soul, and ensuring that you're taking amazing care of *you*, your next most important relationship is the one you have with your partner. Too many people have their children and let their partner hang out on the back burner of their lives while the kids become their focus. Don't do this. Make your significant other the one you nurture, love, and care for first. Show your kids that their parents love each other, and they will know they're safe. They will learn what a healthy, balanced family looks like, and better than all of that, they will carry on the tradition of loving themselves. They will be able to thrive in a strong, happy relationship and will bring up confident, secure young adults of their own. And this is exactly the sort of cycle we want to create. Plus, by being deeply connected, you will create a solid parenting team. You will have more support in your parenting; therefore, you will have more energy for other things, like *sex*. Which, if you haven't figured out by now, you need to have lots of!

Now go out there and grow some warriors. Warriors strong enough to weather any storm that our big, wild, unpredictable world might throw at them. Then sit back and wait for all the phone calls and messages from them, thanking you for loving them enough to be tough on them, and for giving them the real tools they needed to make it out in the world, rather than a corkboard in a childhood bedroom filled with tons of participation ribbons and no coping skills. Give them the armour they need for life.

They're not always going to want to hear it from you; you will get push-back, but remember that you're not here to be your kid's best friend. If you do your job well, then the time when you're their favourite person and they're yours will come around organically. One night I got a phone call from our then twenty-year-old, Mikaela, as she was on her way to initiation night for the new *Kappa*s joining her sorority. She called to tell me she had sprayed the same perfume on herself that I'd been wearing for years, which made her smell like me, which in turn made her think of me and miss me. She called just to share that with me, and to remind me of how long it would be until we next saw each other, which was seven days. She couldn't wait to be home with me, and I couldn't wait for her to be home.

Give them the armour they need for life.

Be the parent who puts in the work to build the relationship that ends up like that. Be their loving warrior and they will become loving warriors themselves. And that, my friends, is how you *keep your cool.*

195

Chapter Eleven

You Survived — What's Next?

YOU DID IT! You survived the first decade of parenting. You not only survived, but you thrived. You raised a decent, likeable, respectful ten-year-old, and you *kept your cool*. Congratulations! I am completely proud of you. I know there were many times along the way when you wanted to throw in the towel, yet you didn't. It's natural to have been out of your depth a time or two, or 1,005! It's also completely normal to have felt unsure of your choices for your kid. I hope I did *my* job during the course of this book: the job of propping you up, of championing you, and letting you know that I have every faith in your success.

If you thought these first ten years had you stumped on occasion, be prepared for an entirely different set of challenges with this next phase of your parenting: the tween and teen years. But don't be scared. Look how far you've come already. You can do these next eight years, I promise. I liken parenting to a video game: you're constantly striving to get to the next level, even though you have no idea what's lurking around the corner, and your heart is always racing with adrenalin. It's always exciting and it's always challenging.

Remember the things that got you to this point: being prepared, being organized, having structure, being unified with your partner. These are the exact same things that are going to see you through any rough patches coming your way through the next eight years. Don't fear — prepare. Don't doubt — believe. You managed the first ten years, you ex-amateur, a person who simply fell in love and wanted to have a family. Now here you are, a decade in. You have ten years of experience under your belt. If you got here with *zero* experience, think about how great you're going to do now that you have that knowledge, that success, and all those victories behind you. Confidence makes us more confident. You're going to kill the game, my friends! I totally know you are. Keep your cool, stay organized, and don't be too proud to say sorry or to ask for help. That's really what parenting is all about. Hell, it's what life is all about. When you're faced with something you know nothing about, or a situation that is out of your scope of knowledge, you can't just turn your back, put your head in the sand and hope for the best. You are responsible for raising this human child into a mighty human adult. You must seek out solutions and support, which is what you did when your child went from truly being a small person to blasting into the double digits. You now have a double-digit-aged person residing in your home. You're entering the tween years. I fondly call this the Jekyll-and-Hyde stage of parenting. You will need to be patient and firm. There will be times when you have a tween who will curl up in your lap insisting on a bedtime story, and there will be other nights when that same young person slams their door and tells you they want to be left alone. It will feel crazy, it will throw you off balance, and it will more than likely cause you to doubt yourself. It made Yannick and I wonder if we had done anything right at all. But we had, and you will, too. Trust yourself, trust the work you've put in, trust the respectful foundation you have built between parent and child, and then march on in this battle ready to produce a well-rounded, strong, intelligent human who will go out into the world and be a wonderful and productive addition to society.

Be sure to continue on in open and honest dialogue with your kid about sex, drugs, and personal boundaries. Remember, just because you've put parental blocks on all the internet devices in your home doesn't mean they aren't seeing and hearing about *everything* everywhere else. Including school. Remember that it isn't "mean" to have access to their social media accounts. You're not here to let your kids do something just because all the other kids are allowed to do it. Don't fall for that bullshit that kids, myself included, have been handing out to their parents *forever*. And definitely don't crumble to parent peer pressure.

> Continue open and honest dialogue with your kid about sex, drugs, and personal boundaries.

This, my friends, is where the real parenting begins. After ten is when the hammer of mindfulness, discipline, and consistency must come down, so to speak. This is when they will test you and their independence the hardest, and it is the time that you *must* mean what you say. The years that are coming down the pike are when all the rules you instilled early on must be enforced. They will test you, and you have to be ready for the test. You must pass it, and the only way you do that is by standing united as parents, being loving, fair, and consistent with your kid. You didn't have them to be their friends; you had them to be their parents, so don't stop now. Many parents I've talked to believe that the younger years are the toughest ones to get through, and in many ways this is true. You're more tired, you run around to all their various activities, you work, you have sex with your partner, you manage your home, and perhaps other kids. Yes, the birth-to-ten years are tough, but the ten-to-eighteen years are the emotionally trying, stay-up-late-waiting-for-them-to-come-home-from-a-party-so-you-can-check-the-whites-of-their-eyes years. These are your frontline, head-above-the-trench parenting battle years, and you must be prepared.

So, bask in the fact that you've come this far, and rejoice in knowing that if you've done the work leading up to this next phase of life, you will have a much more successful time. I'm not here to freak you out; I'm here to be honest with you, the same way I've been honest with you throughout this book. Remember that I'm on your side. I want you to enjoy these next eight years. I want you to write me letters and emails telling me that even though you had challenges and storms with your tween or teen, you're on the other side of it, and that yes, implementing your house rules and seeing them through laid the foundation for a beautiful relationship in which your word was ultimately final, and your kid thanked you for it later.

Our girls still tell us how incredibly thankful they are that we "grounded them" when they broke the rules while they were in their teens. We had no problem taking away their right to the computer and the TV. We cut off one of our daughters' access to her cellphone when she did something particularly egregious (which I won't mention outright, out of respect for her privacy). She got angry when we told her we expected more from her, because we knew she had more to give. She didn't like that we wouldn't let down our expectations even though she was a senior in high school. Those few days weren't easy on us, or our other two girls, but we had to see it through. We had to let her know that we wouldn't be manipulated by her, and that our expectation wasn't meanness, it was love. She came to the realization that we had given her a consequence because we loved her. She understood that we had taken away her privileges because we were concerned she was going down a path that most certainly would have affected her negatively. She understood she was too young to make the choices she was making and to understand the consequences of those choices, because she didn't have the life experience that we had. She couldn't know that what she thought was totally "normal" behaviour ('cos everybody else was doing it) could potentially wreak havoc on her future.

Even today, all these years later, she looks back on how we handled that conflict with gratitude. It opened her eyes and got her to reroute her path. All three of our girls still have a healthy respect for us. Even now at thirty-one and married, twenty-nine, and twenty-three, they would never dream of throwing a party behind our backs or lying to us about anything (or so they tell us). They may keep things about themselves and their lives to themselves, and that's fine. Everybody has a right to privacy. But our girls know that even now, as young women leading their own lives outside our home, we are forever in their corners. They know we will back them in any situation, but they also know we will continue to challenge them and call them to the same level of respect they learned from us as children. Our job as parents is never done, but there will definitely be moments in which we have glorious runs of peace. When those days, weeks, months come, relish it. Enjoy every single minute of it, and praise your kid for being fucking awesome.

IT'S A MARATHON, NOT A SPRINT

By this point in your parenting journey, I'm confident that many things have gone exactly as you planned and that many others didn't, which is how life goes, anyway. I'm confident you did an awesome job of circling the wagons during the storms. You sought support, advice, and guidance from professional people, or others you know and love who had faced similar parenting challenges and came out the other side. All in all, you're doing great, and I am giving you a virtual high-five.

If you've followed my advice, the tween living under your roof is a grounded kid who knows, without a doubt, that you love them. If you've gotten to this part of the book, you will be nodding your head in agreement when I list some character traits you recognize in your young human: a strong sense of self; a tremendous amount of self-confidence; an empathetic nature; and the ability to take the bull by the horns at school, in their extracurricular activities, and in their relationship with you, their parents. You probably have a little bit of an amateur debater — we had two of these, which is a very good thing. You want to encourage that kind of behaviour; it will bring you peace when they go out in the world because you'll know they can handle themselves, stand their ground and meet conflict head on! You have a child who feels confident and trusting enough in their relationship with you to know that they can challenge your point of view on things without being told to "shut up and go to your room."

If you've practised balance in your parenting, then you enter these tween and teen years knowing that no matter what storms come your way, you have the solid foundation of love and respect to weather them all. You trust them and they trust you. You respect them, they respect you, and as long as that is the cornerstone of your relationship with one another, you can't and won't go wrong.

But you must not let up. You must not go soft now. You cannot retreat, thinking your biggest battles are behind you. Don't get lazy or complacent because you might be one of the very lucky ones who has an easy kid. You have to pay attention always; you have to constantly be ready to ask the tough questions about sex, drugs, and bullying. Don't ever be the parent with the rose-coloured glasses on. You know that parent — the one who not only says but believes "*not my kids*, they would never …" Don't be that naive. Be the parent who is able to think, "Hey, my kid *could* be the class bully" or "My kid *could* have weed in their dresser …" Whatever you don't want to believe your kid "might" be doing, check anyway. I mean, what's the worst that can happen? You could be wrong, and they might be offended for five minutes, but trust me, deep down inside they will feel safe, knowing that even though they aren't "babies" anymore, they're still your "baby."

Now, onward and upward, rock-star parents.

This will require wine — for you, not them. Although we did permit alcohol in moderation in our home, the number of times we were called to a party to pick them up for being "blackout drunk" is *none*. But this parenting nibble is not for this book.

xo Shantelle
P.S. Remember to keep having sex!

Further Reading

To read more about the dangers of drinking during pregnancy, visit the Canada Fetal Alcohol Spectrum Disorder Research Network at canfasd.ca.

To learn more about the dangers of electromagnetic radiation and some things you can do to protect yourself and your family, including suggestions for non-DECT baby monitors, check out these resources:

> Radiation Health Risks, radiationhealthrisks. com/7-examples-low-emission-baby-monitors

> Magda Havas, Ph.D., magdahavas.com/safe_ baby_monitors

The CBS News report on kids' screen time quoted in Chapter Seven is "Health Experts Say Parents Need to Drastically Cut Kids' Screen Time," available at cbs-news.com/news/parents-need-to-drastically-cut-kids -screen-time-devices-american-heart-association.

Acknowledgements

IF I TRULY THANK every single person who deserves my gratitude and gushing, it would require a completely separate book. I will instead keep it simple, focusing my attention on the people who are the reason this book exists at all.

To Michele Rubin, my phenomenal, badass, smarter-than-smart rock-star editor at Cornerstones, U.S., who helped me put my words into an actual book form that a publisher would even consider publishing.

To Dundurn Press, specifically Kathryn Lane, who had the balls to publish this "how-to" book: thank you! To Jess Shulman, for being so brilliant and condensing a lot of my rambling to make it concise and smart. You're the best! To Elena Radic, for keeping me on schedule, in a very "keeping your cool" way. And giving me that extra day at the very end!

To every single one of you who bought and read the book, thank you, thank you, thank you.

To the staff at NKPR, for all your brilliant ideas about how to get this book out there and get people excited about it. You're all rock stars. To Michelle for letting me say "no" on some PR ideas and being cool about it. And Rebecca for coming on board in the eleventh hour before your maternity leave was even over, reading the book, and really, REALLY LOVING IT. Your enthusiasm was infectious, and your support for it was second to none. I'll never forget how much encouragement you gave me. And to Natasha (NK), who believed in me when I couldn't. You put your best people on this book, and I will never forget your faith in me. Thank you.

To all my best girls, my ride-or-dies, who always believed in me, who knew that eventually I would end up a published author if I never gave up. You lifted me up on days I couldn't lift myself. I love you, and I thank you for helping me keep my cool for all these years.

To my mother, who taught me how it is possible to sacrifice for the greater good of your kid but still maintain your own identity. Mom, you taught by example how important it is to have a life with your own interests and friends outside of being a mom. I remember the adult dance classes you took, plus the bowling and baseball teams you played on. The fantastic example you set, teaching me that keeping a little sliver of time for yourself is paramount to keeping your cool. Thank you for putting us first. You had so little — little money, little example for how to be a selfless parent — yet you managed it all so excellently, often going without sleep or new things for yourself so that we wouldn't be bullied for looking as poor as we were. You worked long hours, rushing home to get us to dance and hockey, never once complaining about traffic or weather. You cheered the loudest, and clapped the longest. Thank you, and I love you.

To my father, who truly wanted very little to do with me when I was a young girl, and who spent most of my childhood inebriated. I thank you for saying sorry. I thank you for working toward building a bridge of forgiveness, trust, and humility, and for getting sober so that in our older years we could get to know one another. I thank you for teaching me that it is never, ever too late to say you're sorry or to change your ways, and for healing our relationship before dementia came and took you away a second time. I love you.

Yannick. For some strange reason the universe put it upon your heart to fall in love with me when you first met me, when I was a fifteen-year-old Baskin Robbins ice cream girl, and you were the wet dream of Canadian girls the country over. I had no idea. And thank God I didn't know how desired you were, or I might have fucked it all up by wanting you for the wrong reasons. You are the greatest, kindest, most loving man I could ever imagine knowing, and the best father our daughters could ever hope for. I am sorry for all the pain I've ever caused you; I will be eternally grateful for the strong stomach you have had in dealing with me. You are my greatest blessing. Those who know us intimately know this to be a cold, hard fact. Thank you for gifting me with the most important role, the blessing I didn't know I needed or wanted, of being mother to our daughters. I love you more than I think I will ever be able to fully express to you.

Brianna. Wow. What can be said of my beautiful girl? Everything we know about parenting came at your expense. You're stronger than you know, braver than you think, and more lovely, intelligent, and wonderful than I can possibly express. I'm moved to tears when I think about how your choosing me made me into the woman that I became. Thank you for trusting me. Thank you for loving me. Thank you for being strong enough to withstand my weaknesses. I love you deeply, my first-born, and wish you all the blessings that this world can give to you. xoxo

Dominique. You are a dream. Your sensitive, intuitive soul is a gift to me. I know that how deeply you feel can seem like a curse, but trust me, one day soon you will see what an incredible blessing it is. You are my soul girl. I'm so thankful that you picked me to mother you, to guide you, and even more thankful for all the things you've taught me. You, my love, have so much to offer this world. Go boldly and do it. I'm with you, and I believe in you. Thank you for your patience with me. Thank you for forgiving me for all the ways I've blown it with you, and trust that you are my soul, my breath, my reason. xoxo

Mikaela. We weren't looking, yet there you were. Lovely and pure. We were a crew of four. Then you joined the band and life was never the same. Somehow, although you were the youngest, you became the glue that made us a "real family." Ask your sisters: they will attest to the fact that we were good, and then you came along and we were complete. All of our lives were blessed and enriched the day you joined our clan. You're the voice of reason. You're the comedian in trying times. You're the heart and soul at every traditional holiday. Each of us is blessed to know you. I couldn't be prouder of your strength and beauty, and I look forward to watching you set this world on fire. xoxo

When I was a girl of just nineteen, pregnant for the first time, never in a million years would I have guessed that I'd build the family that I have. Each of you girls is the reason our family is what it is, and I hope you know you're the reason, on all my tough days, and there have been many, that I get up in the morning. Thank you, thank you, thank you.